Reclaiming

Yewande Biala is an Operations Specialist in the Bio-pharmaceutical industry who rose to fame after appearing on *Love Island* in 2019. In January 2021, she led a viral conversation about racial renaming and wrote about her experience in the *Independent*, for which she received acclaim and an outpouring of support. Yewande has since written for the paper about colourism and is fast becoming an authoritative commentator on our most pressing issues.

@Yewande_Biala

Reclaiming

Yewande Biala

CORONET

First published in Great Britain in 2022 by Coronet
An imprint of Hodder & Stoughton
An Hachette UK company

This paperback edition published in 2023

1

A CIP catalogue record for this title is available from the British Library

Paperback ISBN 9781399714488
eBook ISBN 9781529389524

Typeset in Bembo by Hewer Text UK Ltd, Edinburgh
Printed and bound in Great Britain by Clays Ltd, Elcograf S.p.A.

Hodder & Stoughton policy is to use papers that are natural, renewable
and recyclable products and made from wood grown in sustainable
forests. The logging and manufacturing processes are expected to
conform to the environmental regulations of the country of origin.

Hodder & Stoughton Ltd
Carmelite House
50 Victoria Embankment
London EC4Y 0DZ

www.hodder.co.uk

For Ayobami Biala

Contents

Introduction

When I was younger and was asked what I wanted to be when I grew up, I often shrugged my shoulders. When asked what type of person I would be proud being of in the future, I would wear a shade of disappointment on my face because I wasn't quite sure. I wasn't sure of a lot of things growing up and had no real sense of direction, but along the way one step at a time, I found my voice – a voice I use today to write. When I was first introduced into the public eye in 2019 on the biggest dating show in the UK, I lost my voice. A voice that I was just finding was now drowned out by journalists, presenters and anyone behind the scenes who had the ability to edit footage, posting whatever version of me made the cut. Anyone who's ever been media trained will know the first thing they tell you is to ignore articles with false headlines and to not add fuel to the fire by giving them a bigger story by just staying silent. But in 2021 I found my voice again through standing up for myself and since then I haven't been able to be silenced. That moment sparked a flame inside me and I found this sudden urge to put my thoughts on paper. And that's what I did in the first two articles I wrote for the *Independent* that were published online in 2021. Since then, I haven't been able to quench that fire. I have no experience in journalism or literature but there is something so liberating about being the narrator of your own story and telling your truth. Something so empowering about letting the words flow through you and explode on the page. Something so fascinating about a blank page becoming flooded with a river of your thoughts and words, forming sentences and paragraphs. Reclaiming every piece of you that was hushed, dismissed and pushed to the side.

My little sister asked me what 'Reclaiming' meant to me and I said it was powerful but difficult to define. Of course, she replied, 'Well, that's not a real answer'. And she was right. Reclaiming means different things to different people, and their collective experiences. For me – and further explored in the essays in this book – it means reclaiming the power to fight for an identity that has been diluted through years of forced assimilation. Reclaiming represents the liberation of my thoughts in all its many facets and intricacies. Reclaiming represents the validity of our collective experiences as Black Africans in the diaspora. Reclaiming represents anyone who is struggling or has struggled to find their voice in a world determined to always speak over them.

It would be a lie to say that I've always wanted to write a book, because I never thought that someone who looked like me with no experience in writing would ever be given a seat at the table. One honest truth I will tell you is that I *love* words. I love how they feel on paper. I love the story they tell and the escape they give you. I love the feeling of the words in my mouth. I love the memories they bring and the air they trap in your lungs right before you're forced to laugh.

Like any new writer, I've questioned my creativity and ability. However, I've enjoyed being the main character of my story for the first time. Writing my own narrative. Being able to create a book about my experience with social media, dating, friendship, body image and more; being able to share my experience as a Black woman and reclaiming that power. I am so excited that I get to publish a book like this, a book I hope a lot of you will relate to and hopefully take something from. I'm still on this rollercoaster journey of life constantly being forced to learn new things against my will, but jokes aside, I am thankful for the journey so far and excited to share some of my thoughts and lessons I've learnt along the way.

I hope it pours into you the same way it has filled me. This has been one of the hardest solo projects I've ever embarked on. If you follow me on social media then you've seen the journey (and GIRL, it was a journey). I think this book needed me as much as I needed it. It acted as a channel towards my future self. Self-reflecting, learning and healing along the way and of course cracking a few jokes here and there, because who likes a boring bitch? NOT ME.

But on a serious note, I've laughed, cried, and gained a few wrinkles along the way. I've had the most amazing time unlocking emotions from all different spectrums and sharing deeply personal moments in my life, all while bringing light to important issues in our society. My essays within this book are raw and deal with a plethora of issues affecting Black women without centring it solely around Black trauma. It's a book I wish I could have given to my younger self, a book that would have saved me years of self-hatred, guilt and confusion.

This book showcases a map of every place I lost myself; it's a collection of all those moments and what I learnt from them. I hope you can learn from them too.

Yours,
Yewande x

Chapter One: Say My Name

'Your name isn't even important. Why are you making such a big deal out of it? Fucking get over it will ya?'

The first and most precious gift your family will ever give you is your name. I was four years old when I realised the importance of names. This realisation happened when we welcomed my little brother into the world. When he was born my parents refused to tell me the name they had chosen for him. So, instead, I had to call him 'Baby'. It wasn't that they couldn't think of a name or that they were torn between choices. It was a sacred moment; they were prophesying all their well wishes for him into prosperity. 'Mummy, what's his name?' I asked her innocently for the fifth time that day while watching this new life they had suddenly become so protective over. 'His name is Baby,' she replied while looking preciously into his eyes and stroking his cotton curls before placing her hand on my shoulder, forcing me to look up at her with a smile.

I laughed. 'That's not a real name.'

'His naming ceremony is next week. The pastor will

come and name him to the congregation. You have to wait till then.'

The following week, I watched how they turned the dining area into scenes from *Hell's Kitchen*. Strange women I had never seen before scrambled around preparing cultural Nigerian dishes in three-foot stainless-steel pots. They stirred the food with wooden spoons with handles as tall as me. I watched how they ran around frantically and shouted at one another with excitement and fear that they would arrive late to church. In the other room my mum and some elders gave the baby his first proper bath, which consisted of heavy scrubbing and what looked like a deep tissue massage. I watched as he wailed but I was told it was necessary. I hid behind all the doors in the house absorbing the commotion that went into preparing for his naming ceremony before I was snatched by an aunty who had been briefed to help me get ready in my white skater dress.

When we arrived at the church, I exchanged excited glances with all the attendees, mainly because I could smell the celestial aroma of the jollof rice that had been cooked to perfection. It exuded the right amount of burnt smokiness, balanced with a spicy aromatic smell when it arrived. I was excited for the celebrations ahead, but I was relieved when I could finally tell the teachers in the school what my brother's name was instead of shrugging my shoulders and saying, 'His name is Baby,' while they laughed nervously, patting me on the back and telling me to take a seat.

I'm not sure how long the ceremony lasted because I was woken up by an angry woman who was outraged that I had balls big enough to fall asleep in a church.

'Wake up! You don't even fear God. Don't you know you're sleeping in his house? Pastor will hear of this. Besides they are naming your brother now.' Her words fired at me in a scorching exclamation of wrath and disdain. I wobbled with shock before joining the rest of the congregation on their feet.

'"Oluwatosin", meaning "God is worthy to be served", "Emmanuel", meaning "God is with us" is born into the family of Mr and Mrs Biala,' Pastor TJ exulted with pure crushing happiness. He requested the church sing it back to him: 'Oluwatosin Emmanuel Biala.' I stood there silently while the whole church chanted his name and rejoiced. My parents' eyes sparkled with pure joy that created a bubble of euphoria around them.

'Oluwatosin,' I whispered to myself and smiled.

Some people move through life without giving their names much thought. Maybe they're vaguely aware of why it was their mother or father's choice or of the shortlist of alternatives being considered before their arrival into this world. Or even what they might have been called had they been born into a different body. For others, a name is something altogether more profound: a signifier of a lifelong link to family history and genetic heritage, or a connection to a wider community. A meaningful ode to their existence: something to be treasured, celebrated and embraced. It wasn't until I was about five years old that my parents explained the cultural and religious significance of naming practices for the Yoruba people (one of the largest ethnic groups in Nigeria) that I belonged to and why my name was linked to my identity.

Writing this chapter forced me to unlock a memory I normally suppress or intentionally keep locked away out of utter embarrassment – roll call. A situation that would unearth a deep sense of uneasiness in me, keeping me rigid in my seat. A memory a lot of you might share, a churned stomach coupled with a wash of anxiety. I had memorised my position in the roll call every year to avoid the echoing laughter of the class as Mrs Finchley struggled to pronounce my name. As I could feel my name coming closer, I would squeeze the bottom seat of my chair. Hoping I would shout 'anseo' to highlight my presence at the right time. But today was different. Mrs Finchley wasn't in, and I would have to wait for this substitute teacher to butcher my name before I could tell her I was here. Names were placed in alphabetical order based on our surnames – this made it worse because the sneers and silent laughs that seemed so loud would last until the last name was called. A wave of sadness gloomed over me for the day and became heavier with every failed attempt she made.

I went home and told my mum that when I grew up and had kids, I would give them European/normative names so no one would laugh at them. My mum sat me down and said. 'You don't know how beautiful your name is'. It was the first time she told me what my name meant or maybe it was the first time I had actually truly heard her. She gently reiterated with a slow smile spread across her face, 'There is power in your name and power in the tongue that speaks it. Raise your head, smile and boldly tell them that your name is Yewande, daughter of Biala.' She could see that I was not convinced as she watched my face slowly contort. I shook my head and wept. She placed her hand gently on my cheek and wiped my tears with her index finger. 'Do you want to hear a story my dad told me about a great historian who kept all the secrets of the Yoruba people and how they choose their names?' I wiped away the remainder of the tear tracks on my face and smiled thinly. She walked across the room and dished out a hot plate of oxtail pepper soup and placed it in front of me. She sat down, crossed her hands slowly and deliberately, took a deep breath in and said, 'Story, story,' and of course I replied 'Stooorryyyy.' She said eloquently 'once upon a time' and traditionally it would always be followed with 'time time'. 'Names are very sacred to Nigerians, especially those from Yoruba-land. There was an elder in

9

our compound who kept all the secrets that were passed on to him from his ancestors,' she attested with a closed-mouth smile.

'What secrets? Tell me!' I interjected impatiently.

'You have to be quiet so I can finish the story Yewande,' she chirped as she looked me in the eye. 'The historian told us that names were given based on circumstances the child was born into. Pre-ordained names Orúko Àmútòrunwá, acquired names Orúko Àbísọ and a Panegyric name Orúkọ Oríkì'.

'Do I have any of these names? I don't understand,' I whined in uncertainty.

'Yes, you have all of them. When you were born, your grandmother – my mum – died, so you never got to meet her, but she came back to me, through you. That's why they called you Yewande, meaning mother has returned.'

'They? Who are they?' I asked, my voice tight with panic.

'We didn't name you. The elders and the people in the compound all gave you your pre-ordained name. Because you were a girl, you were always going to be called Yewande. You were the first girl to be born into the family after my mum passed away.'

I felt my smile harden while I pulled at meat on the oxtail, closing my eyes tightly to avoid the splash back of the peppered soup. My mother laughed and a smile froze on her face before she whispered, 'Ànìké mí.'

'Who's Ànìké?' I asked.

'You are. Your name is Ànìké, meaning birthed to be pampered. A panegyric name your aunt gave you, she would sing praises of her hopes for you. It was a way to imprint you with your complex historical, social and spiritual identities. They would cradle you around the compound and sing songs of appraisal. The last one is the acquired name. Before Christianity, there were many gods that we worshipped. A popular god was Ogun. The historian told us Ogun is the god of iron and, by extension, the god of war and hunting. He was strong and powerful, and many of the other gods feared him.'

'Oh, he sounds so scary,' I mumbled, unimpressed.

'No, Ogun was known to be a messenger between heaven and earth. Ogun was also known to be a fair god who stood for truth and justice. Often people who came from his lineage were warriors and would adopt the name Ogun at the start of their name: "Ogundele", meaning the god of iron has come home. The historian also told us about a beautiful goddess called Oya. Her energy was rooted in the natural world. She was the goddess of thunder, lightning and hurricanes. Fiercely loving but also very unpredictable. She had the ability to change from benevolent and caring mother to a destructive warrior in the blink of an eye.'

'She sounds kind of like you when you're angry, Mummy,' I teased, giggling to myself.

'Yes, she does sound like me. People who worshipped her adopted her name too. However, most people don't worship these gods anymore and have adopted religions like Christianity. Instead, they now replace "Ogun" with "Oluwa", meaning "God".'

'Is that like Tosin's name then?' I replied in a warm tone.

'Yes, it's exactly like that. Oluwatosin. Well done. The historian explained that names were also used to highlight royal descendants among us. Families from royalty would adopt the name "Ade". Male descendants could be named Adewale, meaning "the crown has come home", while girls could be named Adelola, meaning "the crown brings honour".'

My mother placed her hand on my chin, raising my head to meet her at eye level. 'Don't let anyone mock you or your name. It's an insult to your lineage and your ancestors. Your name tells a story of who you are. It serves as a link between you, them, and God.'

Her tone didn't invite conversation. She was stern with her words, commanding so much power in her tone that it forced me to be submissive and accept her words.

My dad walked in with high arched eyebrows. He remained poised and reserved, observing the conversation between my mother and me.

'You forgot so many things,' he said with brisk authority as he pulled out a chair and invited himself into the conversation. 'Listen to me, Yewande. I'll finish the story. Your mother, like many Nigerian women, likes to rush things when it doesn't involve money.'

My mother and I laughed, but we knew there was some truth to his words, so neither of us interjected.

'What your mother failed to tell you was that the great historians told us we had to wait seven days to name a female child and nine days to name a male child. In some cases where there were twins of opposite sex, we would have to wait eight days to name both. But now things are more modernised with equal rights and what your generations calls feminism. So, both sexes are named after eight days.'

'Eight days? That's too many days, Daddy. Why can't they just name the baby straight away?' I contended.

'A child born before the naming is considered a stranger from the ancestral world who has come for a visit. Once the waiting period was complete and the child decided to stay in this new world and not return to the land of the spirits, they would be named. Every child comes from somewhere and is going somewhere. At the naming ceremony there were many symbolic items used to pray for the child. Some of the popular ones were honey, salt and water, do you know why?' he asked, keeping his playful tone.

I looked up at both of them and shook my head from left to right, before remembering my mother hated it when I didn't use my words. 'No, I don't. Why did they use them?' The words came out gentle and soft.

'They used honey to pray for sweetness and joy into the baby's life especially in the distasteful world we live in. Water, because it is pure with no enemies and is needed for survival, symbolising the child will never be thirsty and will have no enemies. Salt, your mum always cooks with salt because she wants the food to taste sweet. The salt is used to symbolise a life filled with flavour and happiness. And that's the end of what the historians from the Yoruba land had to tell us.'

He and my mother both looked at each other and nodded their heads in approval to acknowledge the fact they had recalled the story as they had been told many years ago. My father paused before looking at me and saying 'YEWANDE' in a firm voice with conviction. He only ever said my name like this when I was in trouble, but this time it sounded a little different, or maybe it was the faint smile that played across his lips that gave it away. But it was the way he dragged out the syllables of my name as if every letter meant something.

I learnt a lot from the traditional story my parents told me, but I think I was too young to comprehend its importance. However, it gave me the sense of belonging and pride that I was missing. I didn't say it to them, but

I knew I would never feel embarrassed because someone didn't take the time to learn the correct pronunciation of my name or afford me the grace of asking.

It wasn't until I got older that I realised each sneer, eye roll and huff and puff of '*do you have a nickname? Is there something else I can call you? Why don't we go with your middle name, Elizabeth?*' and '*yeah, I'm not even going to try to pronounce this . . . just raise your hand if you're here*' were all just forms of microaggressions under the ugly umbrella of racialised renaming. A microaggression by definition, according to the Oxford English Dictionary, is a term used to describe 'brief and commonplace verbal, behavioural or environmental indignities, whether intentional or unintentional, that communicate hostile, derogatory or negative attitudes toward stigmatised or culturally marginalised groups.' Microaggression has the prefix of 'micro' attached but anyone who has experienced this type of aggression will tell you they feel like it is anything but small. You don't know how to respond, and you don't want to make it a big deal, but it is. The most common excuse that an aggressor will give is 'oh, I didn't mean it like that', but intent does not equal impact. The issue here isn't unintentional mistakes, but rather how people recover from them. So, when someone doesn't take the time to learn the proper way to pronounce another person's name, or, worse, intentionally mocks it for being 'too difficult' to pronounce or tries to ascribe another name to make themselves feel comfortable, it can come across as malicious. It also evokes a history of dominant groups forcing new names onto people in oppressed groups. If you have known somebody for a long time and are still pronouncing their name incorrectly, guess who has power in that relationship? There is a longstanding history of forced assimilation as a way of maintaining the power structure. Dominant groups dismissing certain names as 'too hard' to spell or pronounce is tied to racism and other forms of oppression. History has taught us that enslaved Africans were forced to answer to their imposed names, impelling them repeatedly to acknowledge their own subjection and powerlessness. The process of un-naming and renaming enslaved Africans was a crucial ceremony as part of an act of possession from the slave master. They were stripped of their names and given new names that had little or no significance to them. Furthermore, enslaved Africans were forbidden from naming their children, although secret naming ceremonies took place, and the children were given 'day names' used solely by the Black people in the community to remind them of their heritage and history. Their children would be named by their slave master. They were given slave names like 'boy', 'girl', 'Slave #1' and 'Slave #2'. Later in that century, they were given derogatory names like 'sambo', 'mulatto' and 'quadroon' when they weren't being called 'nigger'.

16

These terms were dependent on the shade of their skin tone and their proximity to whiteness, as some lighter slaves were blood relatives of the families that owned them – and this still feeds into our society today, but I talk about that some more later. It was very rare for enslaved Africans to be allowed to keep their indigenous names or have them acknowledged.

Earlier this year, I read a book titled *Slave Ships and Slaving*. In it, the author George Dow quotes Edward Manning, a sailor, talking about the slaver Thomas Watson, who once said, 'I suppose they . . . all had names in their own dialect, but the effort required to pronounce them was too much for us, so we picked out our favourite [slaves] and dubbed them Main-stay, Cats-head, Bulls-eye, Rope-Yarn, and various other sea phrases.'

African names were Europeanised once they left the shores, and names like 'Bet', 'Jane', 'Jim' and 'Dick' were given. It's an indisputable fact that forced assimilation and colonisation has had a negative impact on African identity through the obliteration of names. The dehumanisation and oppressive ideology of not allowing a person control over how they want to be named was further amplified when slaves were resold and were now required to answer to multiple names that merely described their physical appearance. Names like 'Wench', 'Darky' and 'Oxfoot' were used to deprive them further of basic human rights and dignity.

After emancipation, renaming constituted an act of eradicating the rupture between the people they had been and the people they were becoming. It wasn't until the end of the American Civil War on the 9th of April 1865 that they were allowed to reclaim their names if they wanted and to legally name their children. Freed slaves chose names like Newman, Liberty and Freeman to assert their independence and status. In the 1960s, freed slaves began to take inspiration for names from African diasporas, which helped establish their sense of self. This prompted the Black Pride movement, where African diasporic people reclaimed their heritage and culture. This was done by adopting names, wearing dashikis and Afro hairstyles. The movement was driven by Black Power leaders who urged Africans to drop their slave names and free themselves from white hegemony.

In 1952, Malcolm Little changed his name to Malcolm X. The 'X' surname represented the identity and cultural heritage that was lost to him as a result of enslavement. Often when enslaved Africans gained their freedom, they insisted on receiving a new name in front of witnesses at a formal event to mark the ending of oppression, the birth of a new person and empowerment. Assata Olugbala Shakur, member of the Black Liberation Army, was born JoAnne Deborah Chesimard in 1947. She chose this name because she wanted it to have meaning and relevance to her life, with 'Assata' meaning 'she who struggles', Olugbala, 'love for the people' and Shakur meaning 'thankful'. Activist, poet and writer Amiri Baraka, who was born Everett LeRoi Jones, is another example. History has taught us the profound meaning of names and how they map one's ancestry. It's important that we praise and honour these powerful names and stories and accept them as a recognition of our African ethnicity.

When I was around eleven years old, I had become accustomed to the idea of rejecting Eurocentricity. While I had a long way to go in finding myself and reclaiming every part of myself that had been stolen in the name of conforming to Eurocentricity, one thing that I no longer tolerated was the deliberate mispronunciation of my name or the lack of respect it had in the mouths of new people. I was asked by Shannon, the receptionist at school, to come to the office my primary. I wasn't being summoned by the principal, so I knew I wasn't in any kind of real trouble and was excited at the prospect of missing class (even if it was only for a couple of minutes).

'You all right, chicken?' Shannon asked.

'Yeah, I'm grand,' I replied, eager to find out why I was there.

'I've just got off the phone with Scoil Naofa. Now they've asked if they could put down your name as Elizabeth Yewande Biala, just so it's easier for everyone,

19

you know.' She looked at me pointedly, waiting for an answer.

Scoil Naofa, the school, were asking if they could change my name to make it easier for everyone. Usually in Ireland the names of schools are not in English, and everyone is expected to be able to pronounce them and keep up with the curriculum, which will also be taught in Irish.

'No, Yewande Elizabeth Biala is fine.' I gave a quick sheepish grin with trembling lips, letting my legs guide me back to the classroom. When I sat down and collected my thoughts, all I heard was that I didn't matter, and I was an inconvenience. From that day, I made it my mission to make sure people knew my name was important – after all, it is my identity.

As I became older and developed my multicultural competence, I decided to stop trying to make others comfortable at my own expense. I was finding my voice, being assertive when my name was mocked or when I was given an uncomfortable look when I corrected them with the right pronunciation. I had familiarised myself with the idea of saying my name twice and quickly rejecting suggested abbreviations and any nickname that was ascribed to me before they had finished the last syllable of their sentence. It's important to recognise that asking for a nickname can feel invalidating; it makes me feel like an inconvenience. Also, ascribing a nickname to a person or participating in racialised renaming can be distressing. You – an oppressor – have stripped me of my identity. You have taken my power in deciding how I should be addressed.

Now that I work in an industry where I meet so many new faces, it's inevitable that I will come across someone who will struggle to pronounce my name. I look at them as they rush the words hoping that I don't interrupt them, avoid using my name the whole day or worse, ascribe me an unwanted nickname that they think is funny by playing on the words already in my name. I remember a time when I walked into my dressing room bright and early, eager to start the day, finish the job and go home. I was met by a member of the production team who had been tasked with scheduling and talent call sheets for the day. He walked up to me, flipped his page and said, 'Interesting name we have here.'

I gave him an unamused soft smile and helped him by pronouncing my name because I'm sure that was his backhand way of asking: 'YE WAN DAY.'

He didn't repeat the words back to me. Instead, he gave me a sarcastic smile and slight shoulder shrug, fostering a 'fuck everyone' energy. I thought it was odd, but I brushed it off. Later that day, the room was filled with whispers and laughter, but it seemed everyone was in on the joke but me. So, I asked them what they had been laughing about all day.

He replied, 'I was just saying your name is just so fascinating. You can do so many things with it.'

I gave him a confused stare.

'Ye wan a burger . . . do you get it?' he continued while laughing hysterically, but I found nothing amusing. The words sounded bitter and cold in his mouth and my irritation amplified.

'Oh yeah, I get it. I just don't think it's funny,' I mumbled dryly.

The silence was deafening.

'I would just appreciate it if you stuck with using my name in the way I introduced it to you. It makes me uncomfortable when you address me with anything other than that.' There was a cool determination in my voice. 'It's just that . . . Well, I've gone through the majority of my life feeling like my name was a burden, and it's not. I love my name. I find it really offensive when there isn't an effort made to get it right or in this case, it's made out as a joke,' I added nervously.

'Oooh no, babe. I didn't mean to upset you. It wasn't funny. I apologise.'

I could see how embarrassed he was as panic rushed through him and a bright pink colour blossomed on his cheeks. He moved his lips at lightning speed, desperately trying to rectify his mistake, his voice croaky from suppressed sobs.

'Thanks for apologising,' I said awkwardly.

Our brief confrontation made me uneasy as always, but I remembered the words my mum kept reiterating: *'there is power in your name and power in the tongue who speaks it. Raise your head, smile and boldly tell them that your name is Yewande, daughter of Biala.'* I left feeling empowered. It felt like reclaiming something I had lost; it felt like coming home.

Imagine living in a world where our culture and heritage were abolished in order to make others feel comfortable. Without an adequate understanding of the elusive dynamics of subtle racism and racialised renaming, microaggressions will remain invisible and harmful to the wellbeing, self-esteem, culture and identity of ethnic minorities. Say my name in one swift note, cherish it, hold it tight and let the melody dance in your mouth before you spit it out.

Usually, when we think of name-based microaggression, we – or maybe I should speak for myself and say, *I*, as a cisgendered heterosexual woman – rarely think of deadnaming as a form of name-based microaggression. But speaking to my manager, Allegra, encouraged me to educate myself on the dangerous and harmful consequences of deadnaming. This is defined by the Cambridge Dictionary as an act of calling 'a transgender person by the name given to them at birth that they no longer use.' Deadnaming, whether intentional or not, can be hurtful, triggering and, in some cases, dangerous. Many transgender and non-binary people choose to change the name they were given at birth because it no longer aligns with themselves or their gender and instead choose a name that is more fitting. Deadnaming signals disrespect and dismissiveness and reinforces the power dynamic in that situation or relationship.

'When I changed my name after my gender reassignment surgery, I felt like me and I needed a name that marked my becoming so I chose Allegra, it's Italian darling, meaning joy and happiness.' Her smile was so infectious, and I could see the words frolicking in her mouth, desperately wanting to be freed.

'I never knew that . . . because I've always known you as Bambi,' I said, eager to learn more.

She paused for a minute, looked down and wore an embarrassed smile. 'Bambi was an easy name to transition into. Bambi has memories of who I was growing up, but Allegra marked who I was all along. Truth is, I was thinking about other people when I chose that name, it was a nickname I already had, and I wanted to avoid a situation where my deadname would accidentally be used so they wouldn't feel embarrassed,' she confided in a measured voice.

I listened as she explained the significance names had to her and how they allowed her to navigate life as a different person, the person she was always meant to be.

'Allegra was always a name my mum would've chosen if I'd been born female, so it was a special moment choosing that name.' Her mouth twitched with a smile. I sat there silent but present.

'What did it feel like reclaiming that name, the first time someone called you by your name, Allegra?' I asked.

'So empowering and so right – it's like when you're trying on dresses for a night out, and you find the one that makes you feel sexy and just fits! I felt like me. I felt like how I should have been my whole life.'

We sat in silence for a while, basking in the moment. I tried so hard to imagine the joy she would have felt telling me about her journey but one glance at her radiant eyes and I knew it was beyond my imagination. The issue in our society is that many people argue that your identity is fixed, which isn't true. Names are identifiers and should have the same fluidity that our identity(s) does. People's failure to recognise and acknowledge this can be very damaging.

'One thing I will say is, during my early stages of transitioning, I was so vulnerable. You could be sitting down in a room feeling amazing one minute and the next someone addresses you by your deadname. You drain. You regress like two, three years. It's that feeling of public ridicule without it being an obvious ridicule. It's gut-wrenching, uncomfortable and something you never forget. There was a guy I knew before and after my transition, we weren't close, but we followed each other on socials, so you know he got the update. He refuses to acknowledge who I am and deadnames me every time he sees me. What irked me the most was that he would say it with a distinct smirk on his face,' she explained in a choked voice.

When someone refuses to acknowledge your identity, whether it's because they don't understand it or they don't agree with it at a basic level, it's just unkind and vile. It's okay to make unintentional mistakes, acknowledge them, apologise and move on, but what you must remember is your mistake has affected someone's confidence and sense of self. What's not okay is to make a joke out of it or invalidate them by saying, 'Oh gosh, I can't keep up'.

While we're on the topic of things not to do, can we address why it's important not to ask for someone's deadname? *'What was your name before?'* Why would you fucking ask someone that? Before what? With every minority, there's always this perceived God-given right from the majority that makes them feel like they can ask any question they want, and that's not the case. Why ask for a name that might've held so many uncomfortable memories for someone when the intention is to never use that name? Asking for it signifies that you don't acknowledge their transition and the new person they've become – that's how much power there is in a name.

Names are prominent identifiers that can often tell the story of one's ethnicity and cultural background. There is a tendency for white European names and whiteness in general to be perceived as normative, whereas racial minorities with names of religious and ethnic origins may be seen as an inconvenience. Many ethnic minority groups are no longer willing to accommodate the dominant white culture at the expense of their own heritage. These incidents may appear banal and trivial but can have a great impact on an individual's emotional state. It's a monumental task to get aggressors to realise that they are delivering microaggressions because it's terrifying to them to realise that they may have biased thoughts, attitudes and feelings against individuals from other ethnic groups. Microaggression is a form of oppression that reinforces existing power differentials between groups, whether or not this was the conscious intention of the offender. Subtle forms of racism, such as microaggressions, can be difficult to identify, quantify and rectify because of their indefinite and unclear nature. While the person may feel insulted, they are not sure exactly why, and the perpetrator doesn't acknowledge that anything has happened because they are not aware they have been offensive. Microaggressions aren't just a racial form of discrimination. There are many marginalised groups of people who are subject to them too, including those from the LGBTQ+ community. Using someone's deadname can make them feel denied of their full existence. It's not up to you to decide what name you want to address someone by. Grow the fuck up and educate yourself #StayWokeBitch!

So, this is what I have to say to you:

Don't ever make others comfortable at your expense. If you've mispronounced someone's name, acknowledge it and apologise. Don't make a joke about them, their name or the situation to make yourself more comfortable' or to lighten the mood. Do ask them what the correct pronunciation is. If you find it difficult to pronounce, break the name down, then say it all together to check that you are pronouncing it correctly. My name is melodious, and it tells a story of where I'm from, so fix your mouth and say it right.

Mistakes are part of life; how you recover from them defines you. Call people by their chosen name – the name they introduced themselves to you as. It's not that hard. No, you cannot call me [insert some other name here].

Chapter Two: Fifty Shades of Black

'SIS! Look at me. As long as your skin is as dark as this, they don't know where to place you in a society that only accepts one shade of Black. PERIODT.

As someone who has suffered at the 'wrong' end of colourism, I thought writing this chapter would be somewhat smooth sailing. Nothing more than a walk down memory lane. Unpleasant nostalgia. The truth is each word I wrote struck harder than a bolt of lightning. They were sharp, cold and angry. I was frustrated, exhausted and enraged that society had let me down! I felt that my people and the culture I am so very proud of had kicked me to the kerb and told me that I 'was the wrong shade of Black'. Of course, no one had used these exact words, but if I'm being honest, I'd rather they did. Instead, they gave me the building blocks to put the pieces together with every microaggression, sneer and rejection. Every whisper was heard, and their voices were clear. Black is only beautiful when it comes in lighter shades.

My experience of colourism is probably no different to that of another Black dark-skinned woman. Colourism in the 21st century is a topic that is quickly swept under the carpet, with some still denying its existence in today's 'post-racial' society. The rise of social media has given birth to people I like to call keyboard gangsters, a group of individuals dedicated to antagonising you on the internet, no matter the topic. Accelerated fingers on keyboards ready to shut you down at any given moment: *'are you man not tired of this topic? Allow it, man. If you wanna be light skinned just say, innit.'*

So, what exactly is colourism? According to the Oxford Dictionary, the term colourism can be described as 'prejudicial or preferential treatment of same-race people based solely on their colour'. There's a parallel relationship between colourism and acknowledging its existence in our community and wider society. Rarely do we ever discuss its complicated history. Understanding this history is crucial to dismantling policies and practices that continue to adversely affect us.

The ownership of enslaved African people by white people regularly resulted in the physical harm and rape of Black women, a concept that is described as 'race mixing' in the 1600s.* This created a social hierarchy

---

* Jones, T., 1999, *Shades of brown: The law of skin color*, Duke LJ, 49, p.1487; https://scholarship.law.duke.edu/cgi/viewcontent.cgi?article=1080& context=dlj

where those who were produced through 'race mixing' had some privileges over those with a darker skin colour. Many slave owners displayed a preference towards lighter-skinned slaves. This was shown by assigning them less strenuous work where they could remain inside, rather than working outside in the horrifying conditions. As time went on, society attached various meanings to these colour differences, including assumptions about socio-economic class, intelligence, physical attractiveness, emotional and mental strength. Those of lighter skin were seen to be softer and were awarded social and economic privileges because of their closer phenotypic resemblance to white people.

When the issue of colourism is spoken about in mainstream media, it's usually narrated by lighter-skinned or mixed-race individuals. Lighter-skinned women have been portrayed in the media as being softer, able to tackle more complex issues, passionate but never angry and, of course, more palatable to mainstream media in the UK – which, let's be honest, is made up of mostly white people. A few examples include Little Mix member Leigh-Anne Pinnock's documentary on racism and colourism titled *Race, Pop, & Power* and *Queer Eye*'s Tan France fronting a new documentary on the issues around skin tone and – wait for it – COLOURISM.

Except this time, I'm the narrator of my own story. No press, no magazines, no quotes – just me, you and the words you read on this page. And, of course, I'm a dark-skinned Black woman.

I'd often daydream of times where I would step into a mystical machine that would shake me all around and spit me out with a lighter, more racially ambiguous complexion with a looser curl pattern and lighter eyes, but my idyllic dreams were often disturbed with one glance in the mirror or a sudden slap by reality, especially on the day I met a young boy called Wale.

'Yo, excuse me miss,' came a voice I heard at a distance, not deep enough to be a man's but also not soft enough to be a young lady. I followed the sound until my eyes found its source. A young Black boy about the age of fourteen smiling right at me with innocent eyes and a charismatic aura. I heard his voice again, only this time closer and with determination. 'Can I speak to you please?'

This was my moment. I could finally live my music video, boy-meets-girl fantasy. Was this really happening? I inhaled the air around me; it was smelling especially sweet that afternoon. I lived in the Irish countryside and was usually greeted with a strong smell of horse manure. I nodded my head firmly and cleared my throat as I processed my thoughts. Hands sweating, I rubbed each finger against another trying so hard not to clench my fists, placing each foot in front of the other, smiling awkwardly at him in an attempt not to scare him off. I had made an effort with my hair and outfit that day. I wore a floral pink dress, one that commanded praise, and wooden cuff bracelets stacked on my wrist that manufactured an echo too loud to ignore. The braids on my head untangled the story of my roots and, of course, Vaseline was smothered all over my face (my mother told me it enhanced my naturally glowing skin).

'Hey,' I said with a weak, trembling voice. Ugh. Why did I say it like that? I had ruined my big moment. I cleared my throat and spoke up, this time accidently shouting: 'Hey!'

He laughed uncontrollably as I stood there awkwardly.

'Hey, my name is Wale. What's yours?'

I smiled anxiously and replied, 'Yewande.'

I knew I had to keep my answers short to limit the chance of embarrassing myself further.

'I was wondering if you could help me out,' he muttered as he rubbed his hands together and smiled mischievously.

'I guess so,' I replied, confused.

'Your friend over there, the light skin one with the light eyes and nice hair. Will she meet me?'

In that moment I froze as I watched the movie scene I had curated in my head crumble into pieces. My music video fantasy was falling apart and suddenly the smell of manure was creeping in, one sniff at a time. What was wrong with my dark skin? Were the coils on the edges of

33

my hair too tight? The gel on the edges of my hair didn't capture each stroke of the brush the way he wanted them to. My eyes didn't tell the story he wanted to read; they weren't light enough. My throat tightened up, eyes filled with tears. Holding each tear back, I smiled and enthusiastically said, 'let me ask her', masking the pain and rejection I felt yet again. The walk back to my friend, Ayo, felt so long, as I dragged myself back, head down, to relay the news of how yet again, she would be chosen.

Ayo was my best friend; we did everything together and were inseparable. I would say things like she was the yin to my yang. Often people would joke and tell me I was saying this the wrong way round because I was the darker friend. At the time, I didn't take much offence to it, but it was something I pondered a lot afterwards. Ayo's favourite season was summer. She always complained of how fair she would get in the colder months as we rarely ever got any sun in Ireland. On the brighter days, we'd play outside and sit in the sunshine, basking in the rays and all their glory, absorbing each ray of sunshine as it joyfully bounced against our melanated skin. I wasn't allowed to stay out for too long because my mother said I would get too dark, and of course we couldn't let that happen . . . though, at the time, I wasn't entirely sure why.

At home, my siblings and I would fight about who had the darkest skin and who was fortunate enough to have the lightest. We were becoming by-products of colonial racism. Each day our minds were absorbing toxic ideologies about beauty and skin colour and from a young age I could see the correlation between beauty and skin tone. The line between beauty and lighter skin was directly proportional, while darker skin was seen as an outlier on the spectrum. It was a phenomenon I struggled to understand growing up and one that didn't seem fair. *'Don't stay out in the sun too long – you'll get darker! Don't use hot water to wash your hands – they'll get darker!'* were constant reminders in my household. Words I programmed my mind to remember for years to come.

The idea of bleaching my skin for the first time came to me when my Aunty Bola came to visit. Now, it is worth saying here that Aunty Bola is not related to us by blood, but as a family friend, the title Aunty marks her status in my life and my respect for her.

'Is your mum at home?' Aunty Bola was here again. She was the type of friend that only came to your house to unpack her problems. I nodded my head while I opened the door wider, encouraging her to come in.

'My mum is in the kitchen. I'll let her know you're here.'

My mother joyfully entered the room, something I never understood. When Aunty Bola came, she always came with so much baggage; it was never a joyful encounter.

'Would you like some pepper soup?' my mother said in her native tongue. I guess you could say this was the

Nigerian equivalent of asking someone if they wanted a cup of tea.

While my mother and Aunty Bola caught up, I sat with them in the living room. My mother was convinced when they spoke in our native tongue, Yoruba, that I didn't understand. Aunty Bola started off by talking about the 'shoe and bag' she bought from Italy and how she couldn't wait to wear it at Shola's mum's birthday party because she had dressed better at hers. Nigerian women's politics. I rolled my eyes and increased the volume of the TV to indicate that they were being an annoyance. However, things were getting interesting. Aunty Bola had started to open up about her husband's infidelities and how she had found one of his mistresses. Now I'm not one to eavesdrop, but they were speaking rather loudly, and my 14-year-old self couldn't resist. It was almost as scandalous as when Kanye West interrupted Taylor Swift's speech at the VMAs that year. Aunty Bola explained how her husband's mistress had fair skin, with looser natural curls in comparison to hers.

'Mummy Yewande, I don't know what else I can do to make this man happy. All these women he seems to be carrying around are lighter in complexion. Maybe me too, I will have to go and buy that fair-and-white cream.'

She was worried that her husband would leave her for this other woman and her only solution was to bleach her skin, using over-the-counter creams you could usually get at any African shop in Dublin. They were so accessible, and the purchase of them was widely encouraged by shopkeepers.

I guess it was to feel more beautiful in a bid to seduce her husband and capture his attention. She had become incarcerated in the perpetual loop of obtaining Eurocentric beauty without a deeper understanding of the message she was sending to me or her daughter at home.

After Aunty Bola had gone home, I revisited my image in the mirror, trying to understand if she was right; did I need to be lighter? Would I be seen to be more attractive if I was? Maybe I just needed to go a few shades lighter. After all there was no one that looked like me on TV or on the front covers of magazines. Even the beauty counters had lighter women. Maybe they were right. They had been screaming, and I was too stubborn to listen. *'Black is only beautiful when it comes in lighter shades.'*

As I grew older and developed my cultural competence, I realised that Aunty Bola didn't know any better and was perpetuating internalised colourist views that were by-products of an environment of colonial racism. Of course, my skin was beautiful, it radiated so much more sitting in the sun absorbing its rays as it bounced on my naked skin. Of course, I was beautiful. I didn't need lighter eyes. My 4C coils were beautiful. Each unique pattern telling a story of its own, a story that I now wanted to hear. Looking back at this series of events with a more educated mind, colourism was at the forefront of my experiences.

The phenomenon of social hierarchy in relation to colourism was something I had to educate myself about from a very early age. I'm sure many of you who are reading this have been unfortunate enough to suffer from the emotional and psychological effects of colourism. For those of you who have been privileged enough not to, you should educate yourself and those around you. Based on historical events, and research into human behaviours, I firmly believe that colourism is deeply rooted in white supremacy, fixed with racial ideologies, rooted in our past centuries' complicated history of colonial racism that have sadly resulted in societal implications in the concepts of social status. Ever heard of the Brown Paper Bag test? No? Okay, sis. In the 19th and 20th centuries, the paper bag method was another way darker-skinned Black people were discriminated against. It was said to be used in the 20th century by many African American institutions such as sororities, fraternities and churches[*] and the outcome of the test could be detrimental to your socioeconomic status. If you were lighter than said bag, hey congratulations, you passed! If

[*] Pilgrim, David (Feb 2014), 'Brown Paper Bag Test', *Jim Crow Museum of Racist Memorabilia*, Ferris State University

you were darker, you failed! It is said that the method was frequently used as a negotiating tool for the admission of Black people into social events, education and even hiring processes. The widespread idealisation of #TeamLightSkinned has led to several biased attitudes and behaviours from people within and outside of the Black community. I don't think I can pinpoint the day I knew that the melanin production of my skin would be one of the biggest obstacles in my life.

As a child, I was always quite timid and shy, mainly because I lacked confidence and was uncomfortable in the skin I was in, attributes that didn't help much when trying to make friends. I mean people weren't queuing up to be my friend, but I wasn't 'uncool' either, or whatever it is that those kids say these days. I was always picked last to be partnered up for school trips, never really invited to birthday parties and wasn't anyone's favourite person to sit beside when the seats for the year were allocated. At the time, I was the only Black girl in my school, so I assumed either no one liked me, or they were all just racist. Things changed drastically when Lola joined the class. It was sixth class and Mrs Keogh had decided that we were all old enough to pick our seating buddies for the year. Everyone had gathered around Lola like a flock of birds. 'OMG, I love your braids, I do,' Kimberly emphasised. 'You're just stunning, you are,' another gushed. I had grown up with Kimberly, from junior infants right through to sixth class, and not once had she ever complimented my braids. I sat on my seat and observed what looked like a circus. Of course, I was itching to introduce myself to Lola, but the thought of being rejected AGAIN had me stuck to my seat like super glue.

'Lola, since it's your first day, who would you like to sit beside?' Mrs Keogh asked.

I slowly dropped my head down to my desk and avoided eye contact with anyone so they wouldn't think that I had hoped that Lola would pick me or that I even had a chance of being chosen.

'Yewande.' *Why was Mrs Keogh saying my name?* I lifted my head up slowly to find Lola pointing at me. By lunch-time we were inseparable.

'Yewande, do you and Lola wanna be on my skipping team for yard time?' Kimberly pleaded during lunchtime. I stood there in complete shock. Why was she even speaking to me? Kimberly was probably one of the most popular girls in school. She rolled with a very exclusive group of girls. The tie-your-hair-in-a-high-ponytail-and-dangle-it-from-side-to-side-as-you-walk type of girls. Always well put together and aced every exam.

'Yeah, I'll ask Lola,' I assured her. Days turned into weeks, and weeks turned into months as we all played together, from hopscotch, skipping, making friendship bracelets out of daisies to even being as mischievous as stealing chalk from

Mrs Keogh's blackboard to play Connect Four in the yard. This was all I ever wanted, to feel connected, wanted and appreciated by the girls in my class.

'Lola,' Mrs Keogh yelled when calling out roll call.

'*A chur i rud Mrs*,' the class announced, an Irish term to indicate when a student was absent.

Lola had chicken pox and would not be coming back for the last two weeks of school. Throughout the day, I heard whispers of the end of the year party that Kimberly was organising, and I was determined to get an invite to this exclusive party – after all we were besties now.

'Heya hun, what time is the party in your gaff again?' I prodded.

'Soz hun, I thought you wouldn't want to go since Lola wasn't coming,' she mumbled.

Her response didn't make much sense, as the rest of the girls were going. I knew I had to assure her that I was buzzing to go.

'*Aahhh*, no, I'd love to go,' I replied.

Kimberly stood there awkwardly with a very distinct smile on her face. The kinda smile you give to strangers who try to converse with you while queuing in Tesco after a very exhausting twelve-hour shift.

'Yewande, unless Lola is coming, you can't come,' Kimberly said with a sharp and bitter tone.

I sat at my desk the whole day trying to understand why

41

Lola received such preferential treatment. While all the other girls in class calculated their love percentage compatibility to their crushes using a very reliable and accurate equation of counting how many times the letters 'L' 'O' 'V' 'E' and 'S' appeared in both their and their crush's name. I reviewed my list over a hundred times. The only difference between Lola and me was that she was at least three to four shades lighter than me, and oh, she didn't fancy Zac Efron. I learnt many lessons that day, and no, it wasn't just that she had horrendous taste in men.

My mean girl experience with Kimberly that was sprinkled with a hint of colourism didn't stop there. I went into adulthood meeting many more Kimberlys who highlighted that my skin tone was just another hurdle I would have to jump over on the racing course that is life as a Black woman. I would have to work ten times harder to be noticed, speak up a little louder to be heard and walk a little straighter to be seen – although six-inch heels would definitely help a girl out. I grew up feeling that it was a privilege for someone as light as Lola to even want to be my friend. I felt I needed her or at least someone with her same complexion by my side to be accepted by society, in the hopes of one day being fortunate enough to be awarded the same privileges. Although I never spoke these words out loud, I believed them to be true. But at that age I didn't understand why. I had internalised the effects of colourism without understanding its complexities and the trauma it would cause as a result. Instead of trying to reprogram my mind to break free from these ideologies, I was now focused on becoming an 'acceptable' standard of beautiful by looking for ways to conform, chasing this 'glow up' that I felt that I needed throughout my adolescence years. I longed to be wanted, desired, appreciated and accepted. As a result, I grew up with feelings of self-hate towards my own skin tone.

I'll never forget the day Black Twitter united to fight the painful and traumatising words that came out of Kodak Black's mouth in an interview he gave in the summer of 2017 as he stated his 'preference' was for lighter-skinned women. Describing dark-skinned women as – and I quote – 'too gutter' and describing lighter-skinned women as 'more sensitive', Black further commented, 'I love African American women, but I just don't like my skin complexion.' If that wasn't enough, he went on Instagram the following day and said, 'It's just not my forte to deal with a dark skin woman,' OKAY SIR. He later admitted that he 'doesn't really like Black girls like that'. I felt sick to my stomach watching the interview. Enraged, I was ready to pick up a pitchfork and charge. But then I remembered we weren't in the 15th century anymore. And in the 21st century, we've learnt to use our words instead (most of the time). So, peeling back a layer of anger and revealing a buried layer of sympathy, I realised that what hurt me was not only his lack of awareness of the poisonous words he was spurting out, but also his own self-hatred that had been rooted in centuries of a painful history. We live in a society where, more often than not, Black's comments would have been laughed at, swept under the carpet and simply written off as a product of internalised racism and self-hatred. However, there are countless instances of artists within the music industry glorifying and reinforcing Black's message in both subtle and overt ways. Chris Brown rapped about his 'yellow model chick' in 'Look at Me Now'. Gucci Mane proclaimed 'yellow everything' including 'yellow bones' on 'Lemonade', and Childish Gambino sang 'Let me pay for what you sip tonight. Mixed girls from Williamsburg, that's my fucking Kryptonite' in 'Put It In My Video', while we had Kanye West holding a casting call for 'multi-racial women only' for Yeezy season four! You can't make this shit up.

While we cannot solely blame influential pop culture for constantly upholding these ludicrous notions, we cannot turn a blind eye to the consequences it has had on society or the way in which it's acted as a catalyst for light-skinned Black women like Beyoncé, Rihanna and Cardi B to sell records. I say this not to discredit these women, their hard work or their immense talent. My view is that when beauty is seen as an indispensable marketing tool alongside talent, beauty standards that are influenced by white supremacy and the approval of the male gaze, it gives heterosexual men too much power to define who or what will sell records and limits the mobility of large groups of women in the music industry. Women who don't look like Beyoncé, Nicki Minaj or Rihanna in more ways than skin tone. I'm talking about women like Nao, Jazmine Sullivan and Ari Lennox.

Earlier, I saw that #StopErasingBlackWomen was trending on Twitter. The hashtag started an important conversation about the unfair lack of representation of dark-skinned Black women on TV. Most importantly, it highlighted how the media was replacing dark-skinned women with lighter-skinned women across all channels of the creative industry. A prominent example that caused uproar back in the day – one I'm still not over – is the replacement of Aunt Viv's character played by Janet Hubert in *The Fresh Prince of Bel Air*. Janet was replaced by a light-skinned actress, surprise. However, the character, played by Daphne Reid, embodied a different persona: the new Aunt Viv wasn't feisty or opinionated, and she didn't have a mind of her own. A stereotype that is way too familiar to me, and I am sure those of you most affected by it.

Some of you reading this who have not been affected by colourism might see these examples as banal and trivial. However, research has linked colourism to lower marriage rates, longer prison sentences, lower incomes, and fewer job prospects.* Don't believe me? Fine, don't take my word for it – Villanova University conducted a quantitative study that examined discrimination based on skin tone (colourism). Their research included 12,000 cases of African American women imprisoned in North Carolina between 1995 and 2005. Results showed that lighter-skinned women received more lenient sentences compared to their dark-skinned counterparts.† Lighter-skinned women were sentenced to approximately 12% less jail time and served 11% less jail time. The study considered the type of crimes the women had committed and their previous criminal history in order to generate like-for-like comparisons. Light-skinned privilege is also apparent in dating and marital rates among the Black community due to the false stereotypes that have been given to lighter- and darker-skinned Black women.

This privilege is constantly echoed in the world of social media. Coming out of the biggest dating show in the UK was supposed to be one of the most joyful moments of my life. Instead, I was greeted with hostility and rejection. Constantly overlooked and ignored, it was a taste of what was to come, and I was terrified. My first point of action was to find a manager, someone who

* 'Colorism', *NCCJ*, https://www.nccj.org/colorism-0
† Viglione, Jill, Lance Hannon, and Robert DeFina. 2011, 'The impact of light skin on prison time for black female offenders', *The Social Science Journal*, vol. 48, pp. 250–258

could guide me and, of course, help me establish a long-lasting career in this new industry. I sat in my hotel room, sent emails and made as many phone calls as humanly possible.

'Hey, it's Yewande. Just ringing to set up a meeting to talk through management opportunities. Are you free sometime this week?' I was always initially greeted with a welcoming tone, but this drastically changed as the conversation progressed and would usually always end with, 'We're actually not looking to sign anyone new, sorry,' only for a 'please welcome our new signing' post on the Gram a day or two later. I had exhausted the very long list of agencies and scouts that had been given to me by ITV producers. I scrolled through Instagram with a very discouraged heart watching the rest of the *Islanders* with lower engagement and followers announce their signings. I swallowed my frustration and was eager to act. I DMed a dark-skinned Black presenter, a Nigerian woman I looked up to, to hopefully give me some advice and direction. We met up in a small cafe near Waterloo and bonded over some cold chips.

'I know how hard this industry is for women that look like us. It took over five years for someone to believe in me and sign me as a client,' she explained, while sipping her coffee. A great sense of sadness flooded my heart, sucking my energy with it as I smiled awkwardly at her. 'I've had to work ten times harder for the jobs I got, and

I'm constantly overlooked for jobs I'm more than quali-fied to do,' she added. The advice she gave me was indis-pensable. 'You're going to get so many nos, so many doors will be slammed in your face, but you'll eventually get a yes and a door will open. When it does, show them what the fuck you're made of!'

I carry these words with me every day when it gets tough, especially at red carpet events, where I am always overlooked in comparison to my lighter counterparts. I notice how eyes linger on them a little longer. How the lenses of the cameras flirt with them seductively. How they are described in the press the following day and how gentle the words are. Most importantly I can see the eagerness and excitement in the eyes of the interviewer when it comes to the lighter women, how their pupils dilate and their eyebrows rise. I have got used to it, accepted it and now look up and grace them with a confident smile.

How did I get here, to a point where I can openly and confidently accept the beautiful skin I'm in? And no, I didn't close my eyes tight and wish for my fairy godmother to vanish all the pain and years of self-hatred away, although I do wish it was that easy. It sure would have saved me a lot of time writing this chapter. Was it through words of affirmation? Some believe that if you speak kind words to yourself, over time you'll simply just believe them. Many people would agree that this alone would be sufficient as a confidence builder. However, I strongly disagree. I do believe that words of affirmation are key to growth and recovery, but there's so much more to it. I believe that the four stages of true self-acceptance are:

- Self-realisation
- Accountability
- Forgiveness
- Self-acceptance and self-love

My self-realisation stage was very late. It wasn't until my first year of university that I began to question the roots of racial slurs about my skin complexion Growing up in a predominantly white area I always felt the need to assert my Blackness in a bid to prove I was pro-Black and to mask the fact that I didn't really know how to be! I know some of you reading this may think, well, that's silly. Of course, you're pro-Black, you're a Black woman. But do we really know what it means to be pro-Black, do we really know what it means to embody it? The sad truth is that many of us don't. I didn't. Being pro-Black isn't just submerging yourself in the culture or fighting for Black rights, it's a lifestyle, a movement and an established order. I wasn't 100% confident in my melanated skin and the features that made me who I am – a Black woman. So, how could I be pro-Black?

'YEWANDE! Come downstairs, NOW.' I could hear

the excitement but also the shock in Faridah's voice as I ran down each step.

'What. The. Fuck?' I managed to get the words out, breathless as if I had run a 100km marathon.

'Fuck! She's had a massive glow up, look at her hair, clothes – aaaahhh, I knew it! She's using cream,' Faridah shouted with excitement as she shoved her phone in my face.

Faridah was the type of friend who was always in people's business and was the first to hear campus gossip. She kept up with the latest trends and prided herself on her appearance. 'Using cream'? What did she mean by that? Well, I guess no one wanted to use the word 'bleaching' or 'skin lightening'. But why was Faridah so excited at this prospect and why was its part of her glow up? Why did Faridah feel like this girl had finally unlocked the Da Vinci Code of reaching true beauty, or at least aspiring to it?

'OMG! She's like three shades lighter. Everything is so blended – I need to ask her what cream she's using, or maybe she's taking those glutathione tablets. Someone told me they are amazing at lightening your skin quickly and evenly,' she explained full of excitement while gazing at her phone, replaying those ten-second Snapchat story clips. As engulfed in them as I am in Beyoncé's Gram pics.

Faridah had dark skin like mine but had been explor-ing ways to lighten her skin for months; it was all part of her plan to achieve the ultimate 'glow up'. I secretly wanted to be part of this plan, but I never said it out loud. Faridah knew this and would always involve me in her plans. I became fixated on the idea that I needed to glow up and was more determined than ever to get there. I guess we were both at the age where attention from young men was imperative to the way we saw ourselves. There were only so many rejections you could handle, only so much 'I think you're fit, but my type is actually light-skinned' or 'I think you'd be so much prettier if you were a few shades lighter' a person could take.

I remember it like it was yesterday – the day Faridah and I decided to bleach our skin. We gathered every cent we had and made our way to the bus station after an intense 15-minute research session on the best lightening products on the market, according to a random Wikipedia search. The plan of action was simple: walk in, buy the products, walk out, go home. The only problem was that it didn't quite pan out that way. We ended up on Moore Street in Dublin, notorious for its abundance of African shops.

'My dear, what can I get for you guys today? Cream? Extensions? We have some lovely wigs, too,' one of the shopkeepers suggested as we walked into the store.

I stood there and smiled awkwardly, looking over my shoulder at Faridah, who was standing behind me with enlarged pupils and worrying eyes, hoping she would interject. She dropped her head quickly while twiddling her thumb.

'I'm okay, Aunty. I'm just looking around. Thank you,' I mumbled.

I felt a sharp pinch on my back followed by a silent whisper from Faridah. 'Ask her about the cream.'

I don't know why I couldn't get the words out of my mouth. On one hand, I knew that by going ahead with this decision I was conforming to the beauty standards that had been shoved down my throat as a result of white supremacy, but my desire to be awarded the privileges that I knew would come with having lighter skin was so much stronger. The women in the store had caught my eyes glancing ever so slightly at the shelves with all the bleaching products. There were so many: lightening, toning and brightening. I guess the term 'bleaching' wasn't very marketable.

'Come let me show you this one. All the girls your age always come and buy from me – it will lighten your skin within one week. You'll be light and beautiful, hmm,' she emphasised while reaching towards the shelf in front of me and picking up a bottle of a cream named 'Diva'.

I stood there nervously evaluating every eye roll, whisper and unwelcome gesture that came from the women in the store. It wasn't that they thought that they were somehow superior to me because they were able to escape the shackles of Western beauty standards. I could tell by the dark knuckles, uneven skin tones and red cheeks caused by the bleaching agents literally stripping away their epidermis that they had fallen for the same tragic fate. They were just Nigerians; Nigerians are very judgemental.

'Will I add this oil too for maximum effect? You will need this soap and night cream too, my dear,' she yammered on while Faridah and I stared at each other from across the room in disbelief. She'd added all the items into the cart and tallied out the total. 'Card or cash, my love?' she shouted while aggressively chewing the gum in her mouth.

When we got home, I rushed upstairs to get ready for bed and carry out my skincare routine, which now had an extra step. I mixed the oil with the cream, just as the lady in the shop had instructed, and left it on the bathroom counter. I looked in the mirror while I let my face air-dry, gripping tightly to the basin of the sink tightly. It lured me in and invited me to look a little deeper, love a little harder and most importantly to take accountability of my actions. I couldn't believe I was really going to go through with it. I had fallen into the same tragic fate as the women I met earlier in the store, I had become a prisoner and been captured and was now in the shackles of conforming to beauty standards set by colonisers. I hated my skin so much that I convinced myself that reducing the melanin that my skin produced was somehow going to make me love myself a little harder. Because maybe just maybe society would finally accept and love *me*. In my self-realisation moment, I couldn't help but also hold a mirror up to society for it to evaluate its contribution to my decision and what its poisonous ideologies had done to me. I had to learn how to love and truly forgive myself. What does forgiveness look like? Taking responsibility, expressing remorse, focusing on repairing the damage I did to my self-esteem and trusting myself. I made the conscious decision to practise self-love. I am beautiful, I am more than enough, and I am perfect with all my imperfections.

Do these issues still affect me? Hell yes!! Do opinions of belligerent individuals have an effect on how I see myself? I'll be damned the day that happens. Working in an industry that's predominantly superficial, one that glorifies Eurocentric beauty and whiteness at its core, one that takes pride in breaking down Black women, I often get a lot of questions about whether I felt that my skin tone had affected work opportunities. The unfortunate answer is, yes! Only last month, I sat in my kitchen on the phone to my lawyer, while I cried silently, clenching my fist and biting my lower lip to help distract myself from the fact that I just wanted to scream at the top of my lungs, each tear continuously falling and flowing as smoothly as the River Nile.

'Do you think I look nice in this picture?' I said,

holding the phone so close to Ayo's face. I always looked for her reassurance. It was one of my favourite pictures; my smile brightened and warmed the room and my complexion was rich. I used to hate smiling; I felt it made my already African nose wider. How foolish was I? My features told a story, a map of where I came from. How could I deny its existence, an existence I came to love?

'Yes, that's one of my favourite pictures of you. Send it to the brand for approval.'

Hours went by, and I finally received a reply. I was so excited to post my image on the Gram, but there was one major setback. The original image I sent was edited. My features were changed, my hair was longer, and I was at least three shades lighter in complexion.

'Their defence is they didn't use a lightening app to edit the picture. If this was brought to court they would drown you in hundreds of thousands of legal costs, whether you had a case or not,' my lawyer disclosed over the phone.

'So, what can we do? What am I supposed to do? Nothing? Am I supposed to just do nothing?' I said, trembling with anger.

'If you release a statement or say anything, they will sue you.' I could hear the grave sadness in his voice as he let the words unravel. I felt a sting of melancholy and confusion. For the first time in eight years, I found myself going back in time revisiting my fourteen-year-old self, standing in the mirror, that day that Aunty Bola had visited, asking myself if I needed to be lighter and why society was so unaccepting of my beauty. What would I have told my fourteen-year-old self back then and, most importantly, now?

That beauty was and is still in the eyes of the coloniser, their inability to accept and appreciate your beauty in all its glory, is not a reflection of you. You are beautiful and perfect with all your imperfections. Sometimes, although we say these words to ourselves, we don't hear them. So, I hope your internal dialogue really takes this in. Let's be real: colourism is still a very real phenomenon even with people still denying its existence in our society today; recognising its implications and the detrimental effects it's had on society is an important factor we must achieve to move forward. If you have been affected negatively by colourism, your feelings are valid; do not let anyone gaslight you and most importantly, something I am still learning how to do, speak up, practise self-love, in a world that has conditioned you to hate your skin. Stop trying to convince people of your worth, their inability to see you is not a reflection of you. Don't let people's insecurities and internalised prejudice become your truth. These are things I am still learning how to do.

Chapter Three:

Blurred Lines and Beauty Lessons

'It's not a bad photo, just slap a filter on it bitch'

Body image. Something about starting this chapter made me really uncomfortable. Perhaps it was the fear of saying something wrong or politically incorrect or maybe it was the fact that I would have to face my own demons, exploring my own insecurities and how they have shaped the person I am today and how society has aided this. I sat in my living room as I sent an email with decisive swiftness to my editor informing her that I would not be writing this chapter. She gently persisted, as is by now clear, so here we are. But what made me so uncomfortable? I owed it to myself to at least find out.

I took a week off writing to dive into my mind a little deeper and explore my thoughts. I had been struggling with what some might call writer's block. Naturally, I threw myself into other aspects of my job – more glitz and glamour. I had a photoshoot the following day, so I decided to take myself to the hair and nail shop. I went into Streatham's finest Afro Caribbean shop to get a restoration hair treatment and get my cornrows fresh and ready for my wigs. The salon reminded me so much of home. Scenes of Nollywood films playing in the background, along with sounds of aunties chirping about business that wasn't their own.

'You shouldn't have left your hair in this long, Yewande. I always tell you.' My stylist Jade couldn't understand why I would leave my cornrows in longer than six weeks when we both knew I would have to face the wrath of that toothcomb brush as she removed each coil that had now tangled and wrapped around the others. While sitting down, hands firmly grabbing the seat for dear life, neck tucked into my chin trying to convince myself that this pain would soon pass, I couldn't help but overhear Shanice, one of the hair stylists, recommending to one of her regulars, sister Linda, what she described as a butt-enlarging cream! I was in the hair shop so of course I wasn't going to mind my business.

'Yuh heard of ah rub which mek yuh batty bigger?' Shanice rambled on, passionately trying to convince Linda why it was essential for her to add this ointment to her beauty regime. Although Linda was polite enough to let Shanice finish her sales pitch, she couldn't shy away from laughing about how ridiculous it all was.

'Aah Shanice, please. The one I have is enough – I'm

even trying to get rid of it,' she hissed as they looked into each other's eyes and laughed hysterically about how crazy it all was. I guess Shanice had to sell her ointments to someone. Gazing at the shelves in the salon, I saw Shanice had managed to stock the beauty counters with solutions to every woman's insecurities, from stretch-mark- and cellulite-reducing creams to weight-gain and weight-loss syrups, breast and bum enlargement creams. You name it, she had it.

'It's crazy, innit? A few years ago, it was all about having the biggest boobs, right?' Jade commented while digging the tail comb into what felt like the epicentre of my scalp's pain receptors. 'Now, nobody cares about boobs. It's all about who has the biggest bum and smallest waist.'

'Dem girl deh love off lip fillah, but it nuh suit dem. Ah fi we sittin dat,' Shanice added in the most ridiculing tone.

The salon suddenly went quiet, everyone went back to their daily tasks. I couldn't help but look at my reflection in the mirror in front of me, naked, bare and unfiltered, staring at my own insecurities but still too scared to explore them more deeply for fear of what I may find. I quickly looked down.

The question rang out loud in my head: 'HOW THE FUCK DID WE BLOODY GET HERE?' From Brazilian butt lifts (BBLs) to fillers, Botox, liposuction, boob jobs and face-altering apps, the list goes on.

Prodding and tweaking every single insecurity we have. Insecurities that were manufactured by society.

I don't think I can remember a time when I was content with my beauty or my body. A time I didn't wish I had bigger boobs, wider hips, a slimmer nose, longer hair or even different-coloured eyes. I guess those are the features of women I saw in the magazines with 'World's Most Beautiful Women' plastered on the cover. It sounds scary to say, but I don't think I've ever been truly happy with the way I look – but has anyone? If I could hear the answers of each of you reading this chapter, I bet the majority would be 'no'. Even now, writing these words, I have to admit that I have book-marked posts, and created a folder on my Instagram saved collection titled 'Glow Up' composed of all the images of invasive and non-invasive surgical procedures and surgeons recommended to me by none other than the infamous Instagram Baddies. Storing them all away in readiness for the moment my balls finally drop, and I have the courage to actually go under the knife. So, no I'm not judging. And if you haven't heard the term 'Instagram Baddie' look it up! Pfft, okay fine, I'll tell you instead. Well at least Urban Dictionary will – it seems to have a better definition. An Instagram Baddie is 'a girl who is always on fleek. Her makeup is effort-lessly flawless, she's up to date on every trend and she never ceases to slay'.

When I came across a study from the Mental Health Foundation* that said young children under the age of six show signs of body dissatisfaction, it didn't shock me. What terrified me was how accurate it was. So accurate that it triggered some of my own experiences in school at the same age. That day when we all stood in line in the yard, full of enthusiasm waiting for Miss Clarke to take us into class. Fighting the electric waves of energy passing through our bodies trying to stay quiet in a single-file line in hopes of being awarded a sticker for our efforts. Katie, who was hyperactive and could never sit still, who we later found out had ADHD, grabbed my bottom lip and stretched it out as far as it went before letting it go abruptly.

'Ouch!' I let out a screech and looked at her with eyes of trembling rage. 'Why'd ya do that for? I'm going to tell Miss Clarke if you don't say sorry,' I blurted out sharply.

Katie stood there with her hands behind her back, moving from left to right in large strides before tilting her head sideways to get a better view and shouting, 'Why are your lips so big and your nose too?'

Sadness and confusion coloured my face. This was the first time I came to compare myself to others in my class.

* https://www.mentalhealth.org.uk/publications/body-image-report/childhood

Were my lips and nose really that big? What else was strange about me that I hadn't figured out? I picked away at myself every day after that, before anyone else could, in a pointless attempt to avoid feeling the first-hand embarrassment and sadness I felt with my encounter with Katie. At least this time I would be prepared. But who set these standards? How was Katie able to tell me at the age of six that the features that make me who I am weren't 'acceptable', not only to her but also to the society we were both living in?

Let's start by figuring out how we got ourselves into this mess, with a deep dive into the evolution of beauty standards – and not just through the lens of a white man as history would have it. If we go as far back as the 12th to the 18th centuries, beauty ideals were predominately based on a woman's potential ability to give birth and to raise a home, so endomorph body shapes were desirable. The ideal woman at that point had wide hips, a wide waist, and a pear-shaped body, coupled with a round face. It wasn't until the 19th century that we saw beauty ideals shift, with women restricting their fullness. I like to call this the early stages of the mass homogenisation of beauty standards in the Western world. It was the evolution of unnatural and sometimes unrealistic body ideals, of teeny-tiny waists and voluptuous breasts, of body shapes that only existed as a result of corsets or other restrictive garments. By the end of the 19th century, a new body ideal had been birthed. Women were more slender; they had sloped shoulders and tapered fingers. An example of this is the painting of Queen Victoria in 1840 wearing rubies by John Partridge.* Towards the early 20th century, these two very different images of full figures and corseted bodies had morphed, creating a new body ideal: slender physique, small waist, wide hips and full breasts. Very realistic? Yes, I thought so too.

At this time, beauty standards were dictated by magazines and Hollywood celebrities. With the emergence of *Playboy* magazine, the idealisation of the so-called 'Playboy Bunnies' resulted in the rise of slender bodies and bust, waist and hip reductions. Women wore low-rise jeans and skirts to accentuate their barely-there waists and flat, long torsos. The proliferation of this aesthetic in mainstream media in the early 2000s and throughout the 21st century ensured the perpetuation of homogenised standards of beauty ideals across Western culture. Internalisation of stringent beauty ideals created room for the objectification and the policing of women's bodies in today's society. Women have desperately tried to conform to beauty ideals for centuries, but as they are ever-changing and often unattainable, it just leaves many

* '1840 Queen Victoria wearing rubies by John Partridge (Royal Collection)', *Grand Ladies,* May 2010, http://www.gogmsite.net/early_victorian_-_1837_ -_18/queen_victoria/1840_queen_victoria_wearing.html

of us feeling inadequate and going to extreme lengths to change ourselves – or at least desiring to.

The biological reality is many women simply cannot have wide hips, a small waist and the attributes associated with being thin without surgical intervention or an extreme exercise regimen. However, women with fuller frames have always been idealised and celebrated in a lot of racialised brown and Black communities. From the beginning of time, Black women have been associated with having fuller frames, especially the lower halves of their bodies. If you weren't thick, you simply weren't hot. Whether we fit the ideal body mould or not, it's the frame we have. I know you've all heard of the viral hashtag that has people by the necks: #SlimThick. And if you haven't, let's talk about it. Firstly, I would like to break this down into two categories. First, there are the natural 'slim-thick' women who have wider hips, thick thighs, big bums and small waists, along with some fat tissue here and there. Second, there are Instagram 'slim-thicc' women, who have what could be considered 'unnatural' body types. Thick thighs, large hips and obnoxiously small waists, ones that make you question the evolution of the human body. To say I didn't idealise these bodies would be a lie. Gworl! I was addicted to Dr Mami's Snapchat stories. For those who aren't ingrained in the BBL culture, Dr Mami is well known in the industry for his cosmetic surgery procedures, and his openness with filming his patients on his social media platforms.

I know I'm not alone when I say that watching music videos on TV was a magical moment, knowing that you turned the TV on at the right time or came back from your bathroom break on the right song. Ingesting the glorious three minutes you were fortunate to watch, blocking out the background noise of a parent yelling at you for sitting too close to the TV. A time before YouTube. It is undebatable that R&B and hip-hop genres helped to mould the culture of the 21st century. From fashion to beauty, whether you wanted to be as thin as Christina Aguilera or have a phat booty like Nicki Minaj or maybe sit somewhere in the middle like Jenny from the Block, repeated exposure to these images via the music industry perpetuated the idealisation of unrealistic beauty ideals. So much so that I had internalised its effects and sexually objectified myself. I convinced myself that because I didn't resemble the images of women that were shaking what their mama gave them in Jay Z music videos, I simply wasn't attractive. And sexy? Girl, totally out of the question. My teenage years and early adulthood consisted of a chest and bum cheeks that were flatter than an ironing board. I equated the attention of the male gaze with not only myself worth but also a measure of my beauty. Society has done a great job at reducing women to objects to be inspected, evaluated and manipulated.

What I find even more disturbing is the brutal pressure from society, in particular the Western demographic, placed on pregnant women. Each year it's becoming more and more stringent. Encouraging women not to gain weight during their pregnancy or at least lose it very quickly and #SnapBack, as if to deny there has been a living human being in their womb for nine months. As if women weren't already held to unattainable standards of beauty and body ideals and now there's a pregnancy ideal. In my opinion, that's the cruellest standard of all.

If I'm being honest, pregnancy scares me. Not because of all the possible complications that could happen during pregnancy but because of the physical changes to my body. Changes that for so many years society has told me to fear and run away from. Changes that are beautiful and natural and map out the precious journey of carrying a child. The stretch marks, weight gain, excess skin, hyperpigmentation and so on . . . The internalisation of this 'thin ideal' and the continuous exposure to cultural beauty ideals has, we know, resulted in low self-esteem and a plethora of body confidence issues for so many.

'Okay, so we've booked you this amazing shoot babe. It's a lingerie campaign. I'll send you the deets on email. Bye!' I was listening to the voice of my booking agent, playing her ten-second voice note over and over again. I let my mind run frantically through all the possible hideous angles I could be captured in. The unflattering images that would be plastered all over social media for the world to see. *'Ughh, I knew it was all editing. She doesn't look like that.'* *'Her body isn't even nice you know – have you seen the new campaign she's just done?'* I could hear the voices of conversations I convinced myself people would be having. The thought of standing in front of a camera – bare, with no control over the images – petrified me, but I couldn't say that to anyone. How could I? All they would hear was someone with skinny privilege complaining about getting her pictures taken. A superficial self-absorbed bitch who hadn't had a reality check. Panic surged through me as I opened the email to look for the date of the shoot. It was in two weeks. I had *two weeks* to change my diet entirely, build muscle and cut down on body fat. I spent every spare minute I had in the gym until shoot day.

The morning of the shoot, I walked on set, eager to get to work, get that cheque, go home and put the day behind me. I overheard one of the models as she whispered loudly that she had stopped eating two days ago and was on a water diet until the end of the shoot. Her words graced my eardrums right at the moment I was entertaining myself with the platter of snacks the client had left in the kitchen, and by that I mean eating as many of them as I could. The other model began explaining that she has small meals throughout the day but stops eating at 4 p.m. sharp. Her judgemental tone made me look over in time to catch them both eyeball-ing my long baguette roll and smiling politely in an effort not to offend me and my decision to stuff my face ten minutes before the shoot. I rolled my eyes quietly in confusion trying to figure out which was worse, teasing yourself until the early afternoon or total deprivation. Of course, these were the thoughts that were cascading through my mind while I picked up my Pret sandwich. I felt guilty but my mouth couldn't resist the succulent taste of that tuna–mayo–and–cucumber baguette.

'Ladies, we'll need you on set in five. Can everyone go to styling and get their first look sorted with wardrobe? Thank you,' Melinda, the shoot coordinator, voiced in the most authoritative tone as she crossed her arms and continued delegating work.

We all walked on set with warm eyes and fake smiles, enough to convince the client to book us again.

'Nice big, wide smiles girlies – we want to see those whites, don't we, Kerry?' Melinda said, chuckling with an emphasised eyebrow raise. As the echoes of laughter flooded the room, my body froze in discomfort. With the first click of the camera, I could feel it stealing my secrets and sharing them with the world. My mind was paralysed but my body was twisting, turning and smiling with every click of the camera.

'Gorgeous, ladies. Pictures are coming out great – ugh

I just love these,' Melinda gushed while staring at the monitor in front of her.

I was worrying about every imperfection, not caring that the majority of people would be able to relate to my insecurities especially with the new body positivity movement, #LetsNormaliseNormalBodies, founded by Mik Zazon, trending on social media. Where people would post relaxed, unedited images of what they would call their true self. I selfishly didn't want to be outed to the world that my airbrushed edited pictures weren't my reality. Like everyone else on social media who hadn't run their picture through Facetune, I too had unwanted rolls, scars, discoloration and stretch marks, and my body isn't flattering in every angle. But my carefully crafted feed of the beauty and fashion influencers I followed suggested otherwise. I don't say this to point fingers, or maybe I do, but it would only be right if I held myself just as accountable for the pollution of images that uphold rigorous standards of beauty on social media.

'That's it, girls. It's a wrap, thank you team. Honestly everyone's done such an amazing job today,' Melinda rejoiced.

I said my goodbyes and was finally on my way home, left in my solitude. I scrolled through my Instagram feed desperately trying to find a meme or post that would lift my mood and have me cracking up in the same way I would after the guy I fancied told a dead joke. Instead, I was met with claustrophobic images of over-edited waists, bended walls, influencers telling me to drink three litres of water for eight weeks precisely to grow my hips and bum, and weight-loss supplements injected with foreign substances. Substances I'm pretty sure hadn't been approved by the FDA that would most definitely have you shitting till the cows came home. Among all these busy images, the two that stuck out to me the most were a photo of a plus-sized model in lingerie showing the reality of a 'normal body' and one of a thin woman also doing the same, only this time in a position that looked very uncomfortable, to highlight her barely-there rolls and next-to-invisible cellulite on her legs with #LoveYourself #AllBodiesMatter. These are the type of images I'm sure you also have come across on social media.

I believe the body positivity movement is empowering, especially in a society that takes pleasure in dictating and policing women's bodies. The movement was started by fat Black women in the late 1960s as what they called 'the fat liberation movement' before it became heavily whitewashed and oppressed the voices of Black women in the movement. The fat liberation movement fought for human respect, recognition, acceptance and dismantling patriarchal oppression over people's bodies and diet culture. As the internet expanded, so did the message of body positivity. It became 'inclusive', but that in turn created an era of watered-down messages. Through the years, the empowering message at the heart of the movement has been diluted and is now reaching a paradoxical situation whereby the body positive movement itself is marginalising the bodies that were previously at its centre. The message that was solely used to advocate for ALL bodies regardless of size, gender, physical ability, identity and race has been employed by brands as a marketing tactic and influencers as a way to raise their profile under the illusion of being 'more relatable', meaning more 'profitable'. I agree that these images are important and have helped a lot of people on social media normalise and accept what they might consider 'imperfections'. The problem here is that majority of my Instagram feed and the diversity campaigns I see now consist of . . . Conventionally attractive white, thin-ish, curvy-ish able-bodied cisgendered women. Don't believe me? Remember that UK brand (who will not be named because I ain't trying to get sued) that created a separate business account to show how diverse and accepting they were of all bodies, by only posting ethnic minority women and what they considered plus-size women (read: a UK size 14 *coughs in disgust*).

So, who's to blame? I'd say it's the fault of social media's most influential people, celebs. The Kardashian/Jenner clan – arguably THE most influential family on social media in the Western world of beauty and fashion. Have they really created unattainable standards of beauty in the 21st century? It's undoubtable that their alleged cosmetics procedures and false advertisements of weight-loss products promote the message that weight loss is synonymous with beauty and this has immensely contributed to the rigorous standards we hold ourselves to today.

I was at an influencer dinner not too long ago. With these types of events, you're never really sure what kind of crowd you're going to get. On one hand, you could really be lucky and the moment you open the door be greeted with a surge of serotonin, squeaky high-pitched voices shouting, 'SIIIIIIISSSS, I KNOW THAT'S RIGHT!' or you could be met with hostility, silent eye rolls and whispers so loud the dead could hear. Unfortunately, it was the latter kind of event that I found myself at.

It only took a few glasses of Prosecco and a shot or two of tequila before Lauren, a blonde girl across the table, who was wearing fake-tan at least two shades too dark for her complexion along with tight ringlet curls courtesy of a ceramic barrel wand, picked up her glass of white wine smudged with the lipstick from her plumped lips and declared angrily, 'I bloody hate trolls you know? Proper scum of the Earth.'

The chatter in the room silenced as the girls decided to lend an ear to what seemed like an open conversation. 'Aah, babe, are you all right? Just block it out, girl. They're not even worth it. Just sad fuckers wanting to feel better about themselves by making you feel shite,' another influencer, Kendell said as she comforted her while holding a rather large glass of red wine to her chest.

'Can you believe it? They accused me of Blackfishing. Bloody insane the lot of them, aren't they?' Lauren said, the words strangled in her throat as she stared directly at me, perhaps looking for validation and words of consolation.

I was the only Black person in the room and was now the centre of attention. But I couldn't give her the validation she wanted or needed. Lauren was indeed Blackfishing. I quickly removed myself from the situation under the pretence of getting myself a glass of Prosecco. While I stood at the bar, thoughts raced through my mind on how best to handle the situation. On one hand, I wanted to ignore it and had hoped that it would be quickly forgotten. But on the other hand, the self-victimisation that Lauren screamed from the tear ducts in her eyes had my blood boiling with anger. When people who aren't educated on this topic speak about Blackfishing, they take a literal translation approach. It does not mean 'they are trying to be Black'. This is an important distinction to make, as this is often dismissed because they do not 'look Black'. Blackfishing was loosely defined in 2018 after a Twitter thread by journalist Wanna Thompson. Since then, mainstream media has shared numerous interpretations of Blackfishing. One that I stumbled across recently that resonated with me was by Leslie Bow; she defined Blackfishing as 'a racial masquerade that operates as a form of racial fetishism . . . Blackfishing situates that style as a commodity. It has the effect of reducing a people with a specific history to a series of appropriate traits or objects . . . Blackfishing is one form of racist love . . . how we appropriate otherness.'

I wanted to tell Lauren it wasn't just that she wore her tan too dark, curled her hair to match that of a 3B curl pattern or that the amount of filler carefully placed in areas of her face stole features not only from Black women, but also from East Asian and Middle Eastern women too. I wanted to scream at the top of my lungs that she was capitalising on Black features while still being structurally and politically white, benefiting from all the privileges that come with remaining white. It's ironic that the modern beauty standard is now shifting and emulating features of Black women. There's an unspoken yet deep desire to have these features and consume them as commodities, but simultaneously there's also a deep disgust for Black people and our humanity. But I didn't say those words. I didn't say anything. Instead, I kept myself company with my social media platforms, watching unlicensed practitioners market face and body fillers with captions 'the Kylie Jenner/Kim Kardashian package . . . get the look' as if these features were theirs to begin with.

The reason this is a problem is that whiteness knows no other position than being at the forefront of what is considered beautiful, the gold standard, and this is evident throughout history. Because whiteness still has the structural power and resources to maintain this position.

One of the many issues I've been working on this year and one of the hardest things I've had to admit is my internal fatphobia and anti-fatness. Fatphobia can be loosely defined as the fear of weight gain or fatness in general. As human beings, we always want to see the best in ourselves and prefer not to be confronted with our own biases or prejudices. Looking in the mirror and checking ourselves can be frightening. Who likes a self-reflection moment? I know I don't. From an early age, I learnt that beauty was somehow synonymous with weight. To be thinner was to be more attractive, respected and desired. I think I was eleven when I first found myself captivated by a makeover show. I was intrigued by the women who would take part, transforming from ugly ducklings to beautiful swans, the most noticeable transformation being their bodies. Popular shows at the time included *Extreme Makeover: Weight Loss Edition*, *The Biggest Loser* and *The Swan*. Women in these shows spent two to twelve months on strenuous workout and diet plans to achieve a size that was accepted by society. In some cases, like in *The Swan*, they underwent numerous cosmetic procedures to modify their appearance. Invasive procedures like liposuction, rhinoplasty, jaw implants, face lifts, the list goes on. With every transformation, I watched people's eyes dilate, eyebrows slightly raise, cheeks elevate, revealing wide gummy smiles, all reinforcing the message that to be beautiful and loved you had to be thin and pretty.

I think subconsciously I carried this message around. It became evident in my early adult years when a friend of mine, who had told me she was determined to lose weight, visited after a couple of months of working out. I opened the door and the first thing I said to her was, 'Wooow Ade, you look great. You've lost *so* much weight.' The minute I finished the last syllable in the sentence I instantly regretted the words. I sat in the living room in great discomfort, replaying our interaction in my head over and over again. It wasn't that she didn't look beautiful before she lost weight or that she needed to lose weight to look beautiful. It was my own bias that made me say she looked beautiful because of it. So, I apologised. 'I shouldn't have commented on your weight when you came in. It was very insensitive and uncalled for.'

We continued our nonsensical conversations and laughed over the simplest things, but it was then I decided I needed to reprogram my way of thinking and dismantle some of the cultural ideologies I had learnt, consciously and subconsciously, over the years.

I've decided to:

- Keep unsolicited health and nutritional advice to myself. If people wanted to know, they'd ask.
- Refrain from commenting on people's bodies, especially weight fluctuations. It is not acceptable to tell someone they have gained or lost weight. Don't be like those African aunties.
- Check your thin 'privilege' and speak up when you see people being fatshamed. Staying silent is contributing to the problem.

I usually refrain from checking the 'request' section of my Instagram DMs as it is normally populated with unsolicited advice, concerns, rudeness and maybe Gary down the road trying his luck after four shots of Sambuca. But one day I saw that I had been greeted with an unusual message from Aoibhe: 'You're so beautiful without the filters. Why do you use them all the time?'

My initial reaction was a sigh of disgust followed by a heavy eye roll while sitting on my toilet seat. I was on my way to pressing the block button, but I found myself stalling and thinking about what she said. It was true; she wasn't lying. I couldn't post a video on my stories without some sort of beauty filter that I had saved from Instagram or Snapchat. It's fascinating how as a society we have become so dependent on these filters. Filters that make your skin tone lighter, alter the size of your eyes, enlarge your lips, make your cheekbones higher and change various aspects of your physical appearance. Beauty filters that are tailored more towards Western standards of beauty, a one-size-fits-all change. And yet, despite knowing this, when I saw myself in this alternative eerie version, my mind still couldn't help but prefer that perfect filtered version.

I saw a video not too long ago, posted by Dr Esho on his social media platforms, that I laughed at. It was about Snapchat dysmorphia. He explained that a client came into his office requesting a filler to make her identical to one of her filtered pictures. Of course, he politely declined, instead offering her counselling advice. That day, as I recalled Aoibhe's words, I looked at the video from a different perspective. It became very uncomfortable and concerning. Not only are these beauty filters detrimental to our self-esteem but also to our self-perception, especially when we start to prefer the filtered version of ourselves, which I did. I can't say I'm never going to use a filter ever again, because that would be a lie, but I'm more aware of its potential damages, not only for myself but in society. So Aoibhe, thank you for the message. I *don't* need to use them all the time; it's time I learnt to see, love and accept my true self.

Like many of you reading this chapter, we are all able to critique modern beauty standards and agree that not only are they damaging but also highly unattainable and the effects they have on us are unforgivable. However, this does not stop us from being bound by them or being motivated to attain them. Despite the conscious reality that occupies our minds, we still force ourselves to believe that if we work a little harder, eat less or more or get filler or Botox, we can achieve these social ideals. Social media has blurred the lines between fictitious bodies and real bodies. We all seem to be stuck in this perpetual loop of constant body dissatisfaction, leading to endless prodding, tweaking and 'fixing'.

Our bodies are instruments for use, not ornaments to be looked at. Developing body image resilience is a continuous ongoing process that we should all be championing and working towards. The first crucial step is to dismantle stereotypes and ideologies of beauty and body image. I want to see true body positivity movements, campaigns in mainstream media, cultural messages and true and genuine representation. Redefine beauty for yourself. Refuse to be defined by other people's notions of beauty.

I know you might not believe me, but you are beautiful with all your 'imperfections'. The scars you have form a map of your journey here on Earth. In a world that wants you to conform to their ideals, REBEL. Be rebellious, be true and be you, because you are more than enough.

Always practise self-love. You are beautiful, you are enough, and you are powerful and worthy of love.

Chapter Four:

'Do I Even Need Therapy?'

*'Perfection is the perfect deception
Not all puzzle pieces fit together perfectly'*

While this is a very delicate chapter, it's important to note that this is an account of my mental health journey. Something I've struggled – and I'm currently struggling – with, like many of you who are reading this chapter. I don't have all the answers, and I don't think I ever will. However, over the years I have discovered different coping mechanisms to deal with my mental health. If you're struggling, please don't be ashamed to seek professional advice; we should all be taking charge of improving our mental health. I'm legally not allowed to give you professional advice, and I'm also not rich enough to survive a lawsuit (matter of fact I'm not rich at all). Now that we've gotten that disclaimer out of the way, welcome to my mental health diary.

Growing up, my mental health was never something

that was at the forefront of any conversation. As long as I was alive and kicking and my biological systems were in some form of homeostasis that was enough for my parents and medical physicians to tick their imaginary checklist that I was in good health. I don't think I can pinpoint the day I knew my mental health was in jeopardy; I'm sure it was an accumulation of things or events that had led to that very moment.

I stayed in bed that morning cradled with sadness, unable to move and smouldering with pain. The worst thing about that day is that it dragged on to night and lingered for weeks. I had let it consume me for so long that I was now so scared to confront the source of my own pain. As someone who has an obsessive personality and is a perfectionist by nature, not being able to control the situation I was in – and further, my emotions – was something that terrified me.

My family, of course, knew that there was something wrong, but no one knew how to deal with it accordingly. My mum tried to get through to me the best way she could, but her efforts were quickly shut down faster than a lioness who had marked her prey.

'Will I make you pounded yam with ogbono soup?' my mum pleaded, offering my favourite Nigerian dish while she sat at the edge of my bed with eyes so precious and sad but hopeful. It had become noticeable to everyone except for me that I lost a considerable amount of weight – ten kilograms, in such a short period of time. At the age of twenty and at 5'6" tall, I weighed a worrying 43 kilograms.

'I'm not hungry. I'm okay, I'm just tired. I'm going to sleep soon.' My replies were short and sharp, leaving no room for a response. I quickly rolled over, dragging the duvet over my head, and closed my eyes tightly and prayed she would leave me to dwell in my sadness. After days of worrying, she called Pastor Jacob to share some biblical scriptures with me and hoped that maybe, just maybe, collectively we'd be able to pray away the sadness. After exhausting all her efforts, she took me to the family doctor, Dr Yvette, to prescribe me some appetite enhancers. Although I'd walked into her office a hundred times before, this time felt different; she stood up as I walked in and looked at me with the same sorry eyes I had seen my mum grace me with. Dr Yvette had known me my whole life, from chicken pox to swine flu, awkward body rashes and even guidance counselling when it came to my university choices. She'd always been there.

'So, Yewande, how can I help you today?' she asked, while locking her hands together on top of her desk.

I refrained from answering and sat in silence until my mum spoke up.

'She's saying she doesn't get hungry. Can we have some appetite enhancers, please?'

'Yewande, I would like to hear from you,' Dr Yvette insisted.

As I looked up to answer, I was met with two pairs of sorrowful eyes. I could feel their heavy hearts, and it was unbearable. *'I just don't get hungry',* I had recited these words so much that I began to believe them myself. The truth? I was starving. I was so hungry that it hurt, but the guilt I felt when I ate was unbearable. Dr Yvette went on and asked a long list of questions I'm sure she had already rehearsed a thousand times before.

She turned to my mum. 'I would really like to refer Yewande to a specialist. I think she might be suffering from depression.'

I'll never forget my mum's reaction that day as she sat in shock and disbelief for a few seconds before telling the doctor in typical Nigerian fashion that there was no need and that it was impossible for me to be depressed at the age of twenty. I was sent home with a few packs of nutritional supplement drinks and a pat on the back. The car journey back home was silent and long. My mum refrained from speaking, which was unusual because we all swore that she loved the sound of her voice.

'Depression? I reject it in the name of Jesus! What are you even depressed about? You have nothing to be depressed about,' were the only words she could string together to make a sentence. Her face contorted as though she was struggling not to cry. I sat there in complete silence. She was right, what did I have to be depressed about? I had a roof over my head, great friends and family, I had just graduated with a first-class degree at the age of twenty. What I soon learnt was that depression doesn't discriminate against class, race or personal or professional achievements.

I went straight to my room and thought about Dr Yvette's questions. The most prominent one was *'why do you think you've lost your appetite? Is it the food? You can talk to me'*. I couldn't bring myself at the time to answer her questions truthfully. But sitting here, raw, vulnerable and open, between you and me, I craved control. Everything around me was unpredictable, uncontrollable, my state of mind and my emotions. I longed for control and the only way I could obtain it was by controlling food. When I ate and when I didn't. I starved myself till the pain was unbearable, at least then I could feel. It was the only time the physical pain matched my mental state, and I was in control. I could *control* how long I felt it for. The hunger consumed me so much that the thoughts that possessed my mind became silent and the only thing I could focus on was the hunger. When I did eat, I wouldn't finish my meals, just so the pain could linger a little bit longer. I hated the fact that consequently, I was rapidly losing weight. I'd become a stranger when I looked in the mirror and was met with a reflection that I didn't recognise. I saw a glint of sadness in her eyes. The more I became acquainted with her, the more I hated her. I felt trapped; it was a fight against mind and body, a battle I was slowly losing.

My unconscious mind was aware I had a problem. I was aware that I was developing some type of eating disorder and I was aware I was in some sort of depressive state. I convinced myself that no one would get it, they wouldn't understand. How could they? They hadn't walked a mile in my shoes, and they never could. As long as I didn't get a professional diagnosis, it wasn't real. I would be fine.

Weeks passed by and things in my life were looking up. I felt more in control and more in charge and most importantly I was in a better state of mind. I WAS IN CONTROL. This meant that I didn't have to worry so much about controlling food; I didn't feel the need to. The depressive thoughts and the sadness I felt had quieted. I could say yes when offered food and I could eat what I wanted and when I wanted. I was ready to confront the stranger in the mirror. The time had come, and the difficult conversation needed to happen.

I was now adamant and borderline obsessed with controlling my physical appearance; I told myself I was taking steps to become a better version of myself, a healthier more polished version. When I starved myself, it wasn't that I was conforming to Western beauty standards in the hopes of becoming a size zero and fitting the mould of the 'perfect body type', or that I wanted to lose weight or was scared to gain weight. I was fighting a mental battle that I nearly lost. *It wasn't about body image*.

3rd August 2016

I started my weight gain journey for the first time. I needed to get to an acceptable BMI or at least a weight range that would stop nosey African aunties from prying into matters that were not their concern. *'Aaah Yewande, are you sick? Is everything okay at home? Why is your mum not feeding you?'* they would ask, eagerly hoping for a negative response so they could have something to gossip about during their weekly catch-ups. Starting was the hardest, but as soon as I saw results, the hard work paid off. I spent hours every day reading research papers about the most efficient way to build muscle and keep body fat as low as possible. I was training five days a week and I loved it. I started setting targets for myself and making rules that I had to follow. I couldn't break a rule; it was important to me. The rules were simple:

- Eat 2,250 calories of clean food a day
- No fizzy drinks, juice or sugar
- No cheat days
- Train five days a week

Simple, right? This was my three-month plan that I extended to six months, and a year later I was still following these rules. I was living a healthy lifestyle. I was in control of my body and my mind. I reiterated these lines to myself every day to justify my ludicrous actions. I looked in the mirror and, finally, I recognised my reflection, I knew who she was and for the first time in years, she was smiling at me. I was ready to ease the rules just a little, one cheat day a month. On my way back from a study session I realised I hadn't hit my caloric intake of 2,250 and by the time I got home, it would be too late to make a meal. I guess my cheat day would come in handy. I went to Charlie's, the best Chinese restaurant in Dublin city centre right on the quay. It had been so long since I stood behind the barricaded wooden shelf and smelled the aroma of soy sauce mixed with Asian spices to order my favourite dish.

'House special fried rice, extra rice, extra soy sauce, extra spicy and, of course, extra veg, to take away please,' the words rolled off the tip of my tongue; it must have been a mind–muscle–tongue–connection. The smell was so intoxicating but in all the best ways. The minute I got home, I devoured my plate so quickly. The succulent taste lingered in my mouth as I walked upstairs to my room. While I sat on my bed gathering my thoughts preparing for an exhausting week, I couldn't help but describe what felt like an overpowering amount of guilt in the pit of my stomach that suffocated me. Followed by heavy throbbing and tightness in my chest. I shouldn't have had that takeaway, there was no need for me to have a cheat meal. Why did I change the rules? I wasn't ready. I felt sick, repulsed by my own actions. I stood up and walked halfway across my room, just far enough that I could see the toilet. I felt a tight knot in my throat and watery eyes. I told myself, just this once and never again. I just needed to get the food out, it didn't belong in me, I wasn't supposed to eat it. I knew if I forced myself to vomit this one time that there would be many times after. It wasn't that I was mentally strong enough to resist the urge. It was just that at that point in time, the mind didn't overpower the body. The voice just wasn't strong enough. I cradled myself in bed and cried myself to sleep.

I knew I had a problem, but where did I go from here?

I kept telling myself I needed someone to tell me what to do, but I did know what to do; I fantasised about it every day: *'eat what you want whenever you want;' 'Don't overthink it; you can't control everything'*. A call that my brain didn't want to recognise. There was no way around it; I needed help, but most importantly, I had to want it. I was stepping deeper and deeper into quicksand, and I was desperate for a helping hand. Mine was Jane, my therapist. She offered an open, unbiased, non-judgemental ear with a warm heart and a welcoming tone. Week by week, we were able to tackle my issues with food, pinpoint triggers and come up with coping mechanisms. Of course, I have my wobbles here and there, and honestly, I do think I'll always have a complicated relationship with food. When I get anxious and stressed, I can feel bad habits creeping in. However, I've learnt to try to find the source of my distress by speaking to someone about them, journaling my feelings, leaning on my support systems and, at the top of my list, listening to music to put me in a good mood.

21st June 2021

I spoke to my therapist about my sister today. For the first time, I spoke about my sister out loud. She died when I was three. I don't have any memories of her, apart from pictures stored in the attic that I try not to look at to avoid upsetting my parents. Just glitches of images and moments captured in my subconscious mind held together by pain and the guilt of forgetting. I don't know exactly how she died, where she's buried or her date of birth. The only thing I know is every day I wake up and imagine what life would have been like to have a sister with an age gap of less than two years. I blamed myself for her death. I know it doesn't make much sense considering I don't know how she died. I grew up with survivor's guilt. Why was it her and not me? Every day, I grieve the memories we could have shared, the jokes we could have whispered to each other in the school corridors and, most of all, her warm embrace, her smile, her sisterly advice and the love and bond we could have shared.

I told my therapist I felt guilty for grieving someone I could barely remember and guilty for nearly forgetting her. Guilty for not being more aware and alert the day she died. When and why I stopped asking for her. I felt anger. Angry that they had stopped talking about her, angry that we didn't celebrate her birthday every year, angry that my younger siblings don't know who she was. For them, she's just a picture in an old photograph, a stranger that faded with every picture they picked up. I had so many questions my therapist could not answer, and I was too scared to ask the only people who could. For many reasons, I was petrified of their reaction. I knew how much I was struggling, and people always say how 'you never get over the death of a child', so I guess I didn't want to feel responsible for the emotions I would unleash. I also think there's a small part of me that was terrified of feeling. If there's one thing I know about myself, it's that my emotions scare me in the same way my younger self was scared of the dark. It was the fear of the unknown and lack of control I would have in both situations. I couldn't control whatever emotion occurred in that moment of time and I couldn't see what was in the darkness. I'd lost control. Most importantly, I was aware of the culture that was ingrained in my household, the same one that was ingrained in our community, the Black community. *What's said in this house stays in this house* married with a culture of avoiding difficult conversations. However, I had promised my therapist I would have this difficult conversation to take steps in healing and truly moving forward. And that is exactly what I did.

Where did this stem from, this culture of staying silent? My personal opinion is that it comes from over 400 years of being kept captive and silenced. Over 400 years of being strong, pushing through and surviving because our very existence depended on it. I'm sure you've heard of or been described as a 'strong Black woman' or a 'strong Black man'. The idea of 'strength' that has carried us for decades but is now undermining an important aspect of our humanity. Humans are not built to be strong and withstand any and everything. We are not buildings; we are emotional creatures. It's okay to feel all the feels, it's okay to want to talk to someone and it's okay to cry. Tears remind you that you're still alive. We've been taught for so many years to keep our trauma locked in because it was nobody's business. To stay silent and be strong. But by staying silent, we continue to critically misdiagnose our mental health issues, lowering our potential treatment options. We stigmatise mental health to preserve our strength only for it to have the opposite effect. I grew up in a Christian home and community. We prayed about things. If there was a problem, there was no prayer that could not solve it. You're heartbroken? Get the Bible and read Psalms chapter 147 verse 3: *'He heals the broken-hearted and binds up their wounds'* and pray about it. You lost your job or you're feeling anxious? *Gwwwooorrrlll*, you better pull up Philippians chapter four verse six: *'Do not be anxious about anything, but in every situation, by prayer*

and petition, with thanksgiving, present your requests to God.'
Read, pray and move on. The Church is a community
filled with people helping and uplifting each other in
hard times, giving advice and a listening ear, but with no
one having real qualifications or education about mental
health. I think the church should take a more holistic
approach to taking care of the mind, body and faith.
Educating the congregation and really lending a helping
hand by reaching out to mental health professionals to
arrange educational seminars. Helping to normalise
these conversations.

7th July 2021

I called my therapist today. It wasn't a scheduled meeting;
I clearly have boundary issues too. I don't remember
always having anxiety. I don't remember always being an
anxious person. It all started spontaneously for me. I mean,
as a natural introvert, I was never really comfortable around
large crowds of people. My final year of university was
when I got my first panic attack. It was an accumulation
of stress I had carried around with me for years with all the
predisposed expectations I had to meet, being the oldest
child. It all just got too much. It started with irregular
palpitations two weeks before my final exams. It was
something I couldn't ignore – it felt as though my heart
just said, 'fuck you, I'm going to take a break and stop
beating for a couple of seconds', then remembered I

would die and worked ten times harder to compensate for its stupidity. However, the anxiety I felt was nothing compared to what was to come after the misdiagnosis I received from my temporary GP right in the middle of my finals. My anxiety got so bad that the girls urged me to go see a doctor in hopes of maybe getting some tips on how to manage it better or maybe some medication if need be. They were right; I couldn't carry on like this anymore, especially in the middle of my finals, what felt like the most important exams of my life.

I explained to the doctor in detail what my anxiety felt like. He took his stethoscope, placed it on my chest and listened to my irregular heartbeat.

He swirled his chair backwards, crossed his arms and paused before looking at me and saying, 'It sounds like you have a heart condition that you were born with, where one side of your heart was underdeveloped.'

I felt a sting of melancholy and confusion while sitting on the stretch bed. 'That doesn't make any sense. I'm very athletic. Surely, I would have known if there was something wrong,' I ranted.

He stopped me abruptly by telling me it was something the doctor wouldn't have picked up at birth and usually becomes apparent in your late teens, which made sense as I was twenty. He prescribed me some medication to ease the symptoms and referred me to a specialist. I walked out of the clinic feeling more hopeless, more anxious than ever and with a bigger problem. I collected my prescription on the way back to uni and told Sarah, who was in her final year of nursing, the news.

'Are you messing? All that from a stethoscope? Did he do a cardiogram?' You could hear the frustration in Sarah's voice.

I shook my head slowly from left to right in disbelief.

'Come here to me, now. Don't be worrying till you get a second opinion, Yewande.'

I booked another appointment with a different GP practice later that week, after my first panic attack. With the new diagnosis hanging over my head, I'd naturally become more anxious, and it took a toll on my body and my mind. It felt like an out-of-body experience; I felt completely powerless, out of control and helpless. I had to act. I went to a practice not too far from my uni. He at least displayed some sort of due diligence and performed a cardiogram along with what felt like an intense game of 21 Questions.

'Everything looks pretty normal to me, Yewande. I have no idea where he got your previous diagnosis from. Looks to me like you just got a bad case of anxiety, which is normal around exams,' he explained. It was revealed that I wouldn't need surgery. I had let my mind run frantically and had read some concerning journals online. Although I'd finally got a diagnosis I could live with, I left not knowing how to actually deal with it. What was

I supposed to do with this . . . anxiety? I assumed after I finished my exams and graduated that it would simply just go away.

However, I soon learnt that anxiety becomes a bad habit – it becomes a way of life. This was my new normal. How I was now as opposed to how I was before. I say habit because I think it's quite addictive. Subconsciously and consciously, we feed on anxiety, creating room for more anxiety, which subsequently leads to us fearing anxiety, which is another anxiety in itself, so it escalates.

After countless sessions with my therapist, to say I didn't know where my anxiety stemmed from would be a lie. As you may know already, I love a little self-diagnosis, so here we go. If you asked me, which no one did, I'd say I suffer from First Born Syndrome. Being the oldest in a family of six, I was raised to be a leader, nurturer and an exemplary role model for my younger siblings. This naturally shaped the person I am today: an overly critical, high achiever, who looks for validation from others. I settled into a job role I didn't apply for, jeopardising my own happiness and accepting an immense amount of pressure and responsibility. I was never one to colour outside of the lines; the whole idea terrified me. Not because I was scared of what the picture would now look like, but that it would now be an image that my parents wouldn't recognise or weren't proud of. My parents would say things like, *'your younger siblings are looking up to you — you have to be a good role model'*. That was when my anxiety started, although I wasn't aware. I collected all the awards I could and strived for the highest in every exam. Although these awards and the recognition were great, I never really wanted them, but I knew how much they meant to my parents. Naturally, I become a passenger in my own vehicle of life. Deprived of the experience to make mistakes, experiment and explore.

I was nominated for Student of the Year every year, but it wasn't good enough, because I never actually won. I never missed a day of school, but it didn't matter because neither did thirty other people in my year. I was intelligent, but it wasn't enough because I wasn't always the smartest person in the room. Even when I graduated with a first-class degree, it was still not good enough because I didn't get the award for outstanding academic achievement in Physical Sciences. The thought of failing an exam and letting my parents down created a shadow of anxiety over me. It was only natural that this made room for Imposter Syndrome, which has no official definition but can be loosely explained as the persistent feeling of inadequacy despite a proven track record of success. I was constantly suffering from a sense of intellectual fraudulence and self-doubt. Basically, I felt like a phoney.

I found myself in spaces I felt like I didn't belong and achievements that I thought weren't mine to claim. I've never celebrated an achievement or milestone because I truly felt I wasn't deserving of it; I'm just waiting for everyone else to figure this out too. It's actually one of the main reasons I've never celebrated a birthday. I feel like there's nothing to celebrate – a whole year but no real achievements to show for it, a reminder that I'm just existing with no real sense of understanding what my purpose is. Jane, my therapist, has helped me quieten down this voice of self-doubt in my head by acknowledging my thoughts and putting them into perspective. Separating fact and fears. Playing on my strengths and weaknesses and overcoming perfectionism. I am an intelligent woman. Sometimes I make mistakes and I may not know everything, but who the fuck does? I'm constantly learning and evolving. That's enough.

6th February 2020

Hair, makeup, camera, action and smile. I perfected the mask I wore to a T. So perfectly that I didn't know how or when to take it off. I had lost myself within that mask. I had lost me. I had lost my smile along with the little happiness I had been holding on to for so many years. How? Well, I quickly blurred the lines of reality and fantasy. I couldn't distinguish what emotions were real and what weren't. When I smiled at the camera-man, whose one job it was to capture my most beautiful and happiest moment, at that time I felt like a liar, a fraud and a deceiver. Radiating joy and exuding happiness but hurting and broken on the inside. I'd already mastered the art of deception with only two months' work experience in my new role as a reality TV star-slash-influencer. As a young woman looking at the glamorous world of celebrities and social media influencers, I always found it fascinating and unattainable. I mean, they were in magazines, on billboards and on the TV, and I guess I was just here, sitting on my dusty bed, putting my feet up after a draining 12-hour shift.

So, you can imagine my surprise when I was told by a casting producer that I was going to be cast in one of the biggest TV shows in Ireland and the UK. I left the show with hundreds of thousands of people not just knowing my name but also believing they knew me as a person from the snippets they had seen every night on TV. Don't get me wrong, I'm not going to sit here and write about all the sad downfalls that come with being a reality TV star, because it wasn't all bad. It was a rollercoaster, a whirlwind, and I loved most of the lifestyle. It had its highs, but it definitely had its lows. So, I do think it's important to be transparent and real about some of the major challenges I faced with my mental health as a result. The hardest thing to deal with was my obsession with people's opinions. I craved control, control over the narrative that people were writing, and when it wasn't aligned with the narrative I created, it unleashed a tsunami of anxiety. One that I had never felt before. With each headline in the press, every tweet sent and every comment written, I was losing more and more control. Social media had created an identity for me that wasn't mine. I felt the need to metamorphosise into this new character they had now created and loved. Losing myself with each like and comment under my Instagram posts. I became obsessed with counting them and equating them to my sense of self and worth. Of course, the gods that control the Instagram algorithm didn't help with this, with each post fluctuating and my engagement dropping drastically. I found myself in a dark place. I know some of you are thinking, *'how do you get to a place where you let your worth be determined by whether a stranger decides to double tap your post or scroll past it?'*. It was easy, I became a product up for sale on my social media and my audience were my customers, buying into me and determining my value with a click of a button. But it wasn't just strangers, it was 'friends': *'Ooh, your last post didn't do well.'* It was brands: *'Well, Yewande's engagement is not as high as we would like it, so on this occasion, we'll have to pass.'* It was my agents, *'You've just got to work hard and see what your audience likes so you can boost your engagement.'* Everything was suddenly about likes, and I craved it. I craved the love that came with it, and I craved attention, and when I didn't get it, it left me deflated.

2nd September 2021

My therapist asked me to name five things I liked about myself. The two that stuck out for her were 'loving' and 'emotionally available'. I used to think that I was something of an emotionally competent and loving person but, looking back, it sounds bonkers considering the fact that I was terrified of my own emotions.

The first question she asked me was, 'Who taught you how to be loving? When we've been talking about family, you speak with little to no emotion.'

I let out an awkward laugh before looking down.

'Do you talk about emotions with your family?' she continued.

As much as I wanted to say yes, the answer was no. If I'm being honest and truthful, I don't think I grew up in an emotional or affectionate household and that accounts for many of the issues that I struggled with growing up with and that I'm struggling with in my early adult years. Three out of my four grandparents died before I was even born, and I don't have memories of my grandfather before he passed away when I was around the age of seven – we lived in different countries. Because of the family dynamic my parents had growing up, not having parental figures – my dad lost both his parents before the age of ten, my mum lost her mum in her teens and her dad before I turned eight – I don't think they ever developed emotionally, and it became evident in their parenting abilities. I hugged my dad for the first time when I was twenty-four years old, when I started developing my own emotional competence. I find it easier building emotional connections with strangers and friends because there's a layer of vulnerability that is locked away.

The look in Jane's eyes was desolate, and her voice was monotone when she asked if my parents had ever told me they loved me. I paused and thought for a while before I nodded my head. There was silence for a while, and I was left alone with my thoughts. It wasn't that my parents didn't love me; we all just didn't know how to handle or communicate our emotions.

She broke the silence by asking, 'Well, how do you know how to be in relationships? How do you know how to be loving? Who are you loving with if you're not loving with family?'

I had no answer, I just didn't know.

When I reflected on things, trying to understand what went wrong and when and how I let things get so bad, the word that kept recurring in my mind was 'strong'. I had built up this facade that I was strong and in control and that's how I wanted to be seen. It had become difficult to let that guard down and just accept some help. Society had always told me that I had to be this strong Black woman, and it was tiring. The assumption is that being a strong Black woman is normal and being anything other than that is weak. We've learnt to normalise our trauma for so long. We've been doing it for over four hundred years. Be strong, push through. The strength is in vulnerability; the danger is trying to push through. Trying to push through with all this compounded trauma. The real crisis is not that we must be strong and push through but that that's what we're expected to do. How do you express pain when you cannot locate the source? I needed to locate the wound, and deal with it accordingly.

14th October 2021

Writing this book has been one of the biggest challenges I've ever faced mentally. I know how important the words are and how powerful they might be. Whether it's being read by my little sister or you, a friend and supporter. I wanted to make you proud – but that is a blessing and a curse. I sat through meetings with my editor and my book agent as they smiled and laughed with joy at targets and marketing milestones. I couldn't shake the sense of fear that took over me as it squeezed all the air out of my lungs. My mind ran frantically with what-ifs and *'you can never do that'* while I gazed into thin air as sadness and doubt combined with joy. I soon learnt that to take power and control, I must acknowledge my fears and doubts.

So here we go . . .

I am terrified that my hard work won't reflect in the pieces that I write.

I am terrified of the book not doing as well as everyone hopes it will.

Above all, I'm terrified of my ability or lack thereof.

What-ifs aren't safe, you don't know what to expect with what-ifs. For so long, I've lived life like I knew what the future held. If I'm living a life that I've already predicted may not even be true, then I'm just going to be paralysed by it. Stuck in my mind. And even if those what-ifs are true, I now know that I will survive and if you're like me and you have those what-ifs at the back of your mind, I promise you will too.

It's time that we start dismantling stigmas about mental health and not just educating ourselves but also our community. If you could have done it on your own, you would have done it already. There's no shame in asking for a helping hand. Mental health stigma is keeping us bound and it's keeping us suffering in silence. I want us to see that we have a way to heal these wounds – the seed we sow today is the harvest we reap tomorrow.

* *If you're in crisis and need to talk right now, there are many helplines staffed by trained people ready to listen. They won't judge you or take any personal details.*

Chapter Five:

The One About "Squad Goals"

'Pinky promise, cross your heart and hope to die?'

Sworn to secrecy by this very oath at the tender age of four, it was a privilege to have been asked to make this promise, a true indication of love, trust and the beginning of a fruitful friendship. For those who don't know me, I'm a rom-com lover. Not just any rom-com lover, *the* rom-com lover, who cries at any given opportunity. The shaking, sniffling, silent crier. I've always found the possibility of it *maybe* being real, magical. Although the romantic relationships were always gripping to watch, it was, however, the foes-turned-friends I loved. The blossoming friendships, the best friends forever and ever till death do them part. Those were the moments that really got me. Conversely, the moments that really broke me were the betrayals, the lies and secrecy. Without a doubt, trust is the most fundamental attribute to have between two people in any relationship. And let's not forget about love, a complex phenomenon, an emotion so deep, it compromises every logical part of you. So powerful that some physicists, like *Interstellar's* Dr Brand, say, *'Love is the one thing we're capable of perceiving that transcends dimensions of time and space'*. If you haven't figured out what this means, that's okay, because honestly, I haven't either, but I thought it was worth mentioning.

However, the two main emotions that are capable of breaking these dimensions are jealousy and betrayal. Emotions strong enough to completely end a friendship. Emotions that in some cases are embedded in the foundation of the relationship or develop as a result of one-sided growth. I've had my fair share of friendship break ups and makeups, and each time, I've grown and learnt, mainly, what I want in a friend and what I don't, while also checking myself along the way.

People say your friends shape the person you are or at least the person you're becoming. There is a saying I have heard time and again that goes something like: *show me your friends and I'll show you who you are*. Ever heard that saying before? A saying that suddenly made me uncomfortable upon reflection. When I fought with my friends when I was younger, my mum would say, *'that's how you know you're good friends, because you fight – you don't agree on everything'*. She explained that because we were still able to maintain our sense of self and voice our opinions, we were in a healthy relationship. Just because my friend's favourite colour wasn't blue didn't mean she wouldn't be my friend forever. However, the older I got, the bigger and more complex the disagreements were. Listening to my mum's voice in my head while also remembering that old saying created a paradoxical effect in certain situations. Sara was a friend I met in my early twenties. We were total opposites, but I guess that was what made our dynamic so special. We brought out the best in each other. She brought out the extrovert in me and I taught her how to practise calmness and patience. The first few months we met; we were inseparable. We told each other everything. Well, almost everything . . . It was a whirlwind. Kinda like when you meet a boy you really fancy, skip the 'getting to know you' bit and just have sex for three months straight without actually knowing anything about each other. Well, that was me and Sara in a platonic way. We had shared so many memories in such a small space of time. I would say things like, *I feel like I've known her my whole life. She's literally like my best friend*', while I looked into her eyes and peed myself laughing from the most ridiculous thing I knew was bound to come out of her mouth. But in all honesty, I didn't actually know anything about her. Or at least things that really mattered, like her political views, beliefs and principles, things that defined a person, in my opinion.

'Babe, let's go out for food. There's this new spot I'm seeing on everyone's Insta story . . . It's in Mayfair and I've booked us a table for six tonight,' Sara rambled on, knowing I wouldn't refuse and would make my way into town, not on time, but I'd be there. After dinner, and a few cocktails away from spilling our deepest most intimate secrets, we were joined by Beth, a girl we both worked with on a project earlier that month.

'Girllss! I thought it was yous. Could hear you from a mile away! I was heading home but I might stay for a bit now. Can I join ye?' she said enthusiastically while slowly pulling out the chair in front of her, suggesting she wasn't she wasn't taking no for an answer. Sara and I exchanged looks before smiling at Beth and nodding our heads in approval.

While hysterically laughing at Sara's juicy sex chronicles, Beth abruptly stopped the conversation by shouting, 'JESUS! Bloody went and only forgot, didn't I. That article you wrote, was amazing! So poignant – well done, girlo.'

'So random, but yeah, thank you,' I replied in a confused high-pitched voice.

We all smiled awkwardly and picked up our cocktails as Sara filled the silence with the most outrageous statement: 'Do you know who I find so funny? Piers Morgan.'

Sara continued cackling at the statement she just made

totally oblivious to the fact that Beth and I were sat quietly with disgust and bitterness plastered on our faces.

'Do you not think he's funny?' she asked, while stretching out her hand and slamming it on the table in disbelief.

'You know I legit think he's racist, Sara,' Beth and I hissed in sync. Not only was I offended and deeply disappointed that someone I called a friend could find a bigot like him funny, but I also could see the admiration in her eyes when she spoke of him. A man who appeared to take pride in tearing down Black people.

I was wrong to think that because we shared so many similarities we would share the same beliefs. 'You do know he referred to numerous Black male artists as thugs, never mind the preposterous things he's said about Black people and the lack of respect he has for us on daytime TV,' I retorted.

I looked at her silently in annoyance, hoping it was enough for her to retract her statement.

Sara looked at me with utter confusion. 'But he's right though, anyways half of the things he says are only to create a social buzz,' she said nonchalantly, while poking the plate in front of her, scavenging what was left of her food.

The silence was as sharp as a paper cut.

'But did you not see the thing he said about the penguins though?' Sara enquired.

'What thing?' Beth replied in a low monosyllabic tone.

'When he said he was now identifying as a two-spirit penguin,' Sara giggled, desperately trying to hold in her laugh.

I couldn't adjust my mind to see things from her perspective and I didn't want to either. Ridiculing a community that had fought so hard to be seen and heard. Although she didn't say these words, I found it concerning that she didn't challenge his intention or his character. I zoned out, still hearing echoes of Beth attempting to educate Sara on the matter and her being reluctant and hard-headed. I couldn't focus on anything but the thunderous roar in my chest.

'Hang on, so would you say you're an ally to the LGBTQ+ community?' I asked sceptically, while leaning forward on my chair and waiting for a reply from Sara, yet secretly sick with fear from what she might say.

'Yeah, of course I am, but I don't agree with it being taught in schools and stuff like that, if that's what you're asking.'

I felt my heart sink and my eyes bored into her like a blast of ice. How could I have gotten it so wrong? *'Show me your friends and I'll show you who you are'*, a phrase I kept hearing over and over again in my mind. I wasn't sure if this was something I could get past, and if I did get past it and remain friends with her, what would that say about my character?

Relationships are never easy and usually involve parties constantly working through persistent problems as opposed to throwing their arms in the air and walking out of the relationship. The issue with conflict or difference in opinions, and sometimes political views, is that everyone views themselves as eminently fair and right and sees the other side as irrational. It becomes about morality and justice, easily making you question your friendship like I did mine with Sara. However, these types of conflicts can't and shouldn't be swept under the carpet. Either you stand up for what you believe in, or you choose friendship. No matter which one you choose, you'll be losing something valuable in the process. Choosing to stay in a relationship where you have opposing views means learning to respect differences in opinions, even if you don't agree. We live in a democratic society, where freedom of speech is encouraged even if it means listening to belligerent opinions. Having friends with controversial views means avoiding heated political conversations and backing arguments with information and presenting them in a constructive and non-judgemental way. And if that doesn't work, *giiirrrlll* accept it and move on. You can't force people to see things from your perspective and sometimes you have to accept the reality that, in a nutshell, your difference in opinion is affecting the relationship and your bond.

But is there a middle ground? I would say yes, and it's learning how to create boundaries in relationships and putting people into boxes. Contrary to popular opinion, boxes aren't always a bad thing. Boxes help us create boundaries and identify people's purpose in our lives. Boundaries can be set at the beginning of a blossoming friendship or, due to a significant shift, new boundaries may need to be set, and that's okay. It's okay to carefully navigate and test safe spaces within any relationship. Not everyone deserves to see all the complex sides of you; we need to remember people need to earn this right. It's okay to have friends merely for social purposes without feeling the need to let them into your personal life or unload your heavy heart to their ears. Letting go of friendships isn't easy; it can be worse than a bad break up. Mainly because the majority of the time you don't see it coming and having to adjust to your new reality can be challenging and very uncomfortable. So, I'm not going to sit here and tell you to completely cut off every friendship you have where you don't agree on a certain topic, whether that's political, religious or moral. However, I am telling you to be more assertive with your boundaries and learn how to compromise without losing your integrity. As for Sara and me, my love for her will never change, but I've learnt to implement distance within our relationship.

THE ONE ABOUT "SQUAD GOALS"

I guess no one really has a guide for the dos and don'ts in friendships, which I find amusing, considering we have a long list of wants and needs in a partner. Things we can and can't stand for, breaking points. *'Nah man, I'm sorry I can never date a man who isn't at least six feet, has a job and is emotionally available, and if he cheats, he's gotta go.'* But if asked what you would and wouldn't stand for in friendships, how quick would your response be? Would it roll off the tip of your tongue as your requirements for a romantic relationship, or would you sit still for a while in confusion. Me? I twiddled my thumbs before I was able to come up with some sort of bog-standard list that was socially acceptable while avoiding selfish wants and needs.

Click, like, follow, comment and share. Welcome to the evolution of social media friendships. From love-struck eyes to fire emojis. Strangers to friends and back to strangers again with just one click of a button – 'unfollow'. Often, I wonder how genuine these social-media friends are, or whether a line should be drawn. Should boundaries be put in place for work friends, social-media friends and your actual friends? I know I'm not alone when I say these lines can easily be blurred. One mishap and I'm quickly reminded with a fiery flame why these boundaries are necessary in maintaining healthy relationships. It's also important to understand that different friends serve different purposes in our lives. While some are destined to teach us lessons, some have blossomed into the most magical things, and some remain a distant memory you refrain from revisiting. After finding myself in the limelight in 2019, social media became my job and, naturally, like any other job in the modern era, I made friends. Only this time, instead of building these organic relationships in the office on a fixed nine-to-five schedule, they were done over the large screen of my iPhone Pro Max, creating a false sense of love and intimacy. I found myself watching heartfelt posts and stories about global warming, challenging racism and homophobia – videos their management concocted as a marketing tool as they portrayed the versions of themselves they wanted others to see.

It wasn't long till I fell for these characters and blurred the lines between 'social-media friends' and 'real friends'. Not only did I have additional friends as a result of my career change, but they were also my work and social-media friends too, three for the price of one. I wouldn't class myself as a person who makes friends easily; I've always struggled to fit into a friendship group. I put it down to my lack of likeability or social skills or the fact that I was an introvert and liked keeping to myself. I would not speak unless spoken to and was more than happy to sit with a group of people without uttering a single word.

However, with my relationship with Olivia, I was

forced to come up with quick snappy sarcastic replies along with dry humour to keep up with her craziness, and I loved it. Olivia was confident on the outside but highly self-critical and self-conscious on the inside, fiery with a loud gob and a belligerent attitude but warm-hearted all at the same time. 'I'd rather have your face than any of these bum bitches, sitting here with a face like a slapped arse,' she'd say repeatedly, as she saw the haunted look of social anxiety in my eyes in large crowds. She grabbed my hand as we catwalked into work events week after week. 'You know you're a bad bitch, right?' she sang while embracing me tightly, withdrawing herself and looking sternly into my eyes. Although I didn't believe any of the words that came out of Olivia's mouth, it still meant a lot that she said them. We were at different stages of our careers; she was on billboards and TV ads, and I was still figuring out what the fuck I was doing. I watched all of her accomplishments with pride and captured every moment to share on social media. I was bursting with pride and joy; we always talked about moments like these, and they were finally happening for her. I celebrated all her wins like they were my own, always cheering louder than anyone in the crowd.

One afternoon, while preparing for a TV appearance in Dublin I got a call with the opportunity to feature in a TV campaign, and Olivia was the first person I called.

'Ahhh guess what *biiitttcccchh*,' I screamed so loud with

excitement that I was convinced the sound vibrations travelled through the phone.

'Spit it out, then,' Olivia squealed with excitement.

'Soooo, nothing's confirmed yet, but I might have just booked my first TV campaign for a hair brand for their Afro-hair range . . . three other girls and I'm the fourth, eeek!' I couldn't get the words out quick enough I was so excited.

'Oooh, why didn't they ask me to do it? I have Afro hair?' she replied, unimpressed.

I felt a great wrench of sadness and said nothing. I've never heard silence so loud before. For a second, I convinced myself that she was right and that I didn't deserve this opportunity, maybe she did.

'Ooh, I dunno. They'll prob be in contact for another campaign,' I mumbled.

After countless instances like this, it became evident that my sole purpose in this friendship was to uplift her and highlight her successes, never to celebrate mine or aid in my growth. But my love for her blinded my perspective and my ability to see things clearly even when she constantly disrespected and singled me out among our friends. So instead of drawing a line and putting boundaries within the relationship, to not only protect my heart but also my peace of mind, I continued giving. Giving my love, time, respect and everything she needed, leaving me feeling unappreciated and undervalued.

My failure to look for red flags in my platonic relationships – or at least to determine what mine were –
made me vulnerable to people exploiting my love, time
and respect. Because I didn't set boundaries, it made me
susceptible to excusing poor behaviour, or maybe I was
hiding from the truth that the relationship I had with
Olivia wasn't one that was equitable or reciprocated.
And by masking this I was enabling her behaviour.

'Ughh, that's just Olivia. You know what she's like,' I
said tiredly to Kelly, while exchanging a look of
frustration.

'I don't know why you let her treat you like that. You
do know she only speaks to you when it's beneficial for
her. Fuck that, I would never let anyone speak to me like
that.' Kelly sighed heavily, exasperated as we revisited last
night's antics.

I tasked myself with hosting a night in with a group of
six social-media girls and influencers. We all met at
events and mainly on Instagram and somehow managed
to remain in contact.

'Bloody hell, Yewande. Didn't actually think you'd
pull this one off,' Hannah said, surprised, while picking
up a handful of salt-and-vinegar crisps with one hand
and a glass of white wine with the other. She took large
strides, walking backwards, and plonked herself on the
couch and crossed her legs.

'Sooo Adam! Ooh yeah, I think I might be pregnant!

And I'm keeping it – tie him down with that one ayyye,' Hannah giggled as she sipped her glass of wine before crashing it on the floor with half of its contents spilling.

'What about Jack?' I asked inquisitively. Her and Jack had been together for four months, both public figures, and had been proudly broadcasting their relationship to the world. 'When did you break up? Are you okay? And who the fuck is Adam?'

'Yeah, that relationship wasn't real; it was just for Insta. Get with the times, girl. I was seeing someone else lawls,' Hannah deadpanned, rolling her eyes.

I was shocked how the words easily tumbled out of Hannah's mouth. Was anything real? I wasn't even sure if our friendship was – after all, I had met her on Instagram, just like Jack.

'Make way bitchesss,' Olivia screamed while running towards us headfirst. She couldn't deal with not being centre of attention longer than five minutes. 'We need to be more active on socials. Has anyone posted anything on Instagram? Let's take a picture.'

We all took turns taking photos, so everyone got one they were in.

'Stunning babe,' Kelly gushed over my shoulder, while looking intensely into my eyes.

'Lemme see. Don't post that till I see it,' Olivia demanded while fidgeting anxiously on the chair. I pointed the phone towards her face, waiting for a shrug of approval; it was the only picture one of the girls managed to take.

'Don't post that. I don't like my toes,' Olivia said dismissively.

'Babe, they're fine. Aren't they, girls?' I tried to persuade Olivia.

'If you post that, I'll get all my followers to attack you. I have millions,' Olivia said, as she continued scrolling on her phone in the most dismissive manner.

We all chuckled awkwardly, and I smiled uncomfortably, waiting for the moment to pass, but I could see behind the mask of pity and second-hand embarrassment everyone wore on their faces. The social rejections I felt in that moment translated to physical pain. My chest tightened and my heart palpitated. It didn't take long for me to realise I was in a one-sided relationship.

Like in any relationship, communication is essential, not just to avoid misunderstandings, but also as it's important to have open and honest dialogue about sensitive issues and set clear expectations. Open and honest communication isn't always about who's right and who's wrong but more a way of constructively exploring differences, seeing things from different perspectives and being open to listening in a non-judgemental manner. Actively reaching out to communicate with someone who is unable to utilise these tools will result in a conversation that is disconnected, closed off and in some cases explosive. And that's exactly what happened when I was forced to confront Olivia at our mutual friend's birthday party. Generally speaking, I really hate confrontation, for many reasons. Namely fear. Fear of the conversation getting heated and not being able to find the right words to navigate myself through the storm. Fear of finding the right words to navigate myself through the storm and losing a friend in the process.

I walked into the party with clammy hands and a dry throat, knowing I would be reunited with Olivia. We hadn't spoken in months, apart from the odd Instagram notification with love-struck eyes to keep up appearances. I got tired of having to walk an extra mile and never being met in the middle. I had completely stopped contacting her and, in a way, it was the confirmation I needed when my phone didn't ring and our conversations on WhatsApp were pushed further down. I, of course, greeted everyone when I walked in, including Olivia.

'The fuck is that energy? Don't say hey at all if you're going to say hey to me like that,' Olivia screeched in a childish fit of anger, demanding an explanation for my closed-off and cold greeting.

'I don't know what you mean. I'm just giving you the same energy.' My reply was cold and sharp.

We exchanged bitter looks throughout the day before she looked at me and yelled out in annoyance, 'Well, if you've a problem, spit it out then!'

'I feel like you don't value our friendship or respect me as a friend. We haven't spoken in two months. Two months is a long time – I'm basically a new person,' I said sharply.

'Okay.' Olivia shrugged in a moment that demanded so much more. 'It's not even that deep. Get over yourself. I don't talk to Kelly every day – you don't see her whining and making a fuss of it,' she added before calling her boyfriend and telling him how I was making such a big scene, her eyes tracing the shadows of my body as she emphasised her words.

But that was a lie, she spoke to Kelly almost every day. I tapped through their stories on Instagram, watching their private jokes, and wondered why no one thought to invite me. It seemed childish when I said it out loud but what I craved most from our friendship was intimacy, loyalty and a love that wasn't selfish or with conditions.

When she got off the phone, I chose to be the bigger person. I told her I wasn't mad that she hadn't called me for two months, I was upset that she hadn't called me at all, ever. The relationship relied on me making all the calls, sending all the texts and making plans for things she might or mightn't show up to. It became draining making excuses for her behaviour and feeling the need to always please her was exhausting. Olivia hadn't developed the ability to be empathetic or selfless. She didn't have the emotional maturity to listen, quieten down her inner mental monologue and be present in a moment that required vulnerability.

We both left the party not resolving any of our issues. I reached out the following week as my agent had informed me about filming commitments we had together, and I didn't want any awkwardness on camera. We resolved our issues while sitting outside a small cafe in Oxford Street basking in the sunshine and warm July weather London had to offer. While picking up my glass and looking into Olivia's eyes, I somehow knew it was the last time this conversation would happen. I knew it was the last time I would be reaching out to fix a relationship that was broken and flawed but still one I held so close to my heart. And quite frankly, I knew she really didn't give a fuck and wasn't empathically intuitive enough to recognise this.

Losing a friend can be cataclysmic but letting go of a meaningless connection is healthy and mentally beneficial. The relationship you should be investing the most time in is the one you have with yourself. You need to ask yourself what the cost of being in this relationship is. Is it your peace of mind, do you have to lose yourself in order to co-exist peacefully and is it costing you your happiness? If the answer is yes, then it's too expensive. Friendships are supposed to make life a beautiful meaningful journey. Choosing yourself above all is never something that you should feel guilty about. Olivia and I had a toxic relationship, but it didn't stop me from feeling nostalgic about the precious unforgettable moments we shared. Breaking up with her stole a piece of my heart that held happiness, laughter, pure love, anger and disappointment. A piece that is missing. A piece I remember is lost when I hear her laughter, see her smile or feel her pain. I moored all the memories we could've made and grieved for someone I loved and lost all while learning a valuable lesson.

Pain lets us forget that when one door closes another will definitely open. I met a stranger at a party a couple of weeks ago who told me he wasn't sure why people were so scared of making new friends.

'Losing people is just part of life's cycle of progression. Yes, it sucks but fuck it! Smile at every stranger you meet,' he crooned, gently leaning on my shoulder, close enough that I could taste the remnants of food in his mouth and smell the smoky odour of the nicotine that lingered on his breath.

I smiled slightly and nodded my head gently in approval. He stared at me, desperately trying to dive into my thoughts, squinting his eyes in hopes that it would be magically written on my forehead.

He gasped in some air before adding, 'You know what! There are just so many stories to hear and so many people to hear them from. Why stop yourself from hearing other people's stories, just because the one you were listening to has come to an end?'

He looked away for a couple of seconds before joining the rest of the guests outside for a glass of wine and a round of social smoking, leaving me to ponder on the words he had left. Not every friendship needs to be rekindled. Closing a chapter allows you to focus on the other chapters in your life you might've neglected and establish new meaningful connections. Letting go of an expired or toxic friendship is an indication of growth, even if it doesn't feel like it at the start.

When I was younger, an old man in the pub once told me that a friendship older than ten years was a friendship that would pass the test of time. People seemed to either say wise or foolish things when they were handed a pint of Guinness. Today, I can confirm he was a wise man.

'*Sé an taithí an chíor a thugann an saol do dhuine maol,*' he whispered to himself while picking up his carefully dispensed pint. An old Irish proverb that means: '*There is no doubt that a man who has lived long enough to lose his hair will know a thing or two about life.*'

For years, friendships have been considered cultural and not biological. Valued but not invaluable. If you're lucky enough to have met your forever friend in your adolescence years, I don't need to explain how precious these types of friendships are. Kemi is the reason I don't act a damn fool on social media. She's responsible for the best parts of me. She's the reason why I went on a dating show that most of you know me from, the reason why I wrote my piece on racialised renaming and ultimately the reason why you're holding this book right now. Of course, I wrote these words, but without her support I would never have finished or maybe even started this journey of reclaiming. We underestimate the power of positive female voices and friendships in our lives and how paramount they are to our success and growth. How they fundamentally shape the person we are.

We've both watched strangers walk in and out of each other's lives, picked up the pieces and mended each other's broken hearts all while watering the seeds that were planted in the relationship. Kemi has the super-human ability to see potential tsunamis before they happen.

'There's just something about that girl I don't like . . . just be careful. I know you don't like to see the worst in people. But you get carried away too easily . . . This girl is not your friend. Yewande, not everyone is your friend,' she lamented.

I could see the pain in her eyes as she said these words for the hundredth time, knowing she'd have to deal with the brunt of whatever fallout had resulted from me not taking her advice. That was the best thing about our friendship, we both put each other first.

The most amazing thing about finding your person is

being able to flow in harmonious synergy, knowing what true happiness and love entails. My dad, like many, used to say there's no such thing as a best friend.

'Do you not know you came into this world alone, and you'll leave alone?' he would say while crossing his arms and laughing to himself, wondering when I would wake up from my fantasy. 'So, if Kemi said jump into fire, would you jump?' he'd ask with puzzled eyes and a curious contorted face.

My answer back then was a silent 'yes', but I was too scared to tell him that because I knew he would say I was a fool. But fifteen years later, I'm wise enough to scream 'YES'. When I was twelve, I assumed he was referencing real flames. But what he was talking about was trust – how much I trusted her and how much I valued her judgement.

I'm ashamed to say that I've lost some forever friends because of distance, my reckless attitude and continuously telling myself that drifting relationships was just part of life's spring-cleaning cycle. More often than not, it's due to weak communication, unsolved issues and laziness on both sides. Long-lasting friendships require continuous self-examination, emotional growth and nurturing. I put the drift down to the pandemic, time, distance and work. Pretty much everything but me, without realising that I was the problem. My actions were a catalyst for the space that grew between us. I was engulfed in my self-righteous, holier-than-thou bullshit act and somehow convinced myself that if there were hiccups in the relationship or breaking points, they were not a result of my doing but were down to Niamh's behaviour. Niamh was one of my best friends. We met at university, and she was the first person to speak to me or involve me in class discussions.

'Do you wanna come out tonight then?' I heard an unfamiliar voice, but I knew the words were meant for my ears. My eyes rotated around the room desperately trying to locate its source. It landed on a green-eyed, pale white girl with terrible muddy dark-brown roots and vibrant auburn hair.

'Sorry, what's your name?' She was apologetic and sincere in her tone.

'Yewande. My name's YE-WAN-DAY,' I enunciated slowly, looking everyone in the eye because I knew they were curious.

'I'm Niamh. A few of us are heading to Karma tonight for freshers. Pre-drinks at mine around ten. Do you wanna come?' Niamh asked.

Of course, I said yes and four years later we were both science graduates with memories of drunken adventures wandering the streets barefoot, one-night stands and secrets about who was shagging whose girlfriend in the student accommodations in Willow Park.

A day didn't go by that we didn't speak. Well, days when she wasn't in a relationship or wasn't seeing someone seriously. Those days normally dragged into weeks and months and eventually I would get a phone call to inform me about what crazy argument she'd had with her partner and why their relationship was ending. I took no pleasure in seeing her heartbroken, but I was happy to have my friend back. Instead of telling Niamh how neglected and isolated I felt when she was in her relationships, I suppressed it, consequently resulting in distance. Preventing me from addressing the problem and instead projecting my own preconceptions of what she thought of me and our relationship. Allowing my negative feelings to view her actions and lack of communication as selfish.

But after all this, spending months ruminating over my actions and how I handled things, analysing friendships that I had lost because I was projecting my own preconceptions, misreading cues and misinterpreting conversations, it became evident that the situation could have been avoided. One phone call, one text and one conversation. Although we stopped talking because she stopped reaching out, I stopped reaching out too. Maybe she felt the same way I did, maybe she thought I just didn't want to be in her life anymore. It took an Instagram post from Niamh for me to realise how I'd lost one of the most important friendships in my life. It was an engagement post; she was getting married. She had found The One. A moment that we planned, a day I was supposed to be involved in, a memory we were both supposed to share. All rendered to a single Instagram post. Till this day I haven't been able to bring myself to like that post. I was happy for her, but in a selfish way, it made me sad about all the time that I missed and about not making the time to call, to check in, to be less selfish and let go of my narcissistically self-absorbed tendencies.

There comes a time where you decide what battles you're willing to fight and what battles just aren't worth it! And this one was. I picked up my phone for the first time in nine months and as soon as I heard her modulated voice everything seemed to naturally fall into place. We spoke about wedding plans and the proposal. It went without saying that we both knew I was never going to be as involved as we had always talked about. But that one call saved a friendship that to this day I am still working on. Communicating, no longer blocking thoughts in hopes that time will mend itself, we have a mutual empathic understanding of what is required in our relationship for it to work effortlessly. I've decided to use every perceived rejection as a reminder to start reaching out more. Drifting can be quite natural but there are some friendships that are too good to ever let go.

From what I've learnt from all of this, here's my advice.

All of this taught me to throw away the idea that you don't need to work on a friendship and that if it's meant to be it will be. I've realised that every friendship is a relationship that needs to be watered with the right ingredients to grow fruitfully. There is no such thing as a perfect friendship, but there is such a thing as a good one and that takes work from both sides. Real meaningful friendships consist of pure love. A love that is patient. *'Love does not envy, it does not boast. It is not proud, it is not rude, it is not self-seeking. It is not easily angered. It keeps no record of wrong.'* (Corinthians 13:1). So, I won't let a friendship that's worth fighting for go because we both temporarily got lost in our own ego and pride. Sometimes love needs time before finding its way home again.

If any of this is chiming with you then I encourage you to learn to create boundaries in relationships and always protect your heart. I'm starting to do it with mine, and I'm seeing a difference already. Don't be scared of letting go of a love that is not serving you because you're too scared of starting over again. Take accountability for what you might have done to negatively impact your friendship and learn from your mistakes. In my experience, this is the best way to grow and make sure all of your future friendships are strong and meaningful.

Chapter Six: *Typing* . . .

'Honestly, I can't live without my phone. Twitter is legit my Sky News.'

What's the first thought that comes into your mind when I say Instagram, Twitter, TikTok? Okay, what about when I say social media as a whole? Toxic, unrealistic, the ghetto? Or would you say it's a balanced escape from reality, a perfect equilibrium designed precisely to bring people together? Sharing memories, political views and injustices, with a few drops of created realities to formulate a balanced equation. When the topic of social media is discussed, it normally invites negative connotations and self-help speeches usually starting with 'Why social media is ruining your life . . .'. But you know what's worse – telling people you work on social media for a living. Dare I even say the word 'influencer'. I know, right! First world problems.

I'm a firm believer that life is all about creating a unique balance; no one thing is ever bad for you – everything in moderation. Apart from drugs. Don't do drugs, kids. Because of this I take extra care with how I spend my time on social media, what images, messages and politically biased information I ingest consciously and subconsciously. I like to think that social media can be split into two divisions, kind of like yin and yang, inter-connected and counterbalancing.

I would like to think that in my twenty-six years of life, I've seen and heard the most ridiculous things being posted on the internet. But no one could prepare me for a tweet that read, 'Can anyone help me find an estate agent for metaverse? I'm trying to buy land'. I must be missing something here, because we are living in a time where people are buying, renting and selling virtual land using real money! In ten years I'm either going to be gutted that I missed out on a great investment opportu-nity, like I did with crypto, bitcoin and NFTs. Or I'm going to laugh about what a tragic phase it was on our digital timeline. Living in what I would describe now as the peak of our 'digital age'. I find the world around me is rapidly changing and I haven't had the chance to catch up. So, what exactly is the new digital world we are unlocking called the metaverse and why is it such a big deal? Metaverses are nothing new, we played My Scene. com for those of you who are old enough to remember, that was sort of a metaverse. A virtual reality experience, inspired by augmented reality, that creates a unique space that mimics interactions from the real world. Except back in 2007, when we were picking clothes and accessories and living in these metaverse houses, it was for free. Now in 2022, there are so many different metaverses, with one of the most popular ones being Decentraland. Ethereum, the native cryptocurrency of the platform, settled $2.5 trillion worth of transactions in the second quarter of 2021*! Okay, I'm going to have to say that again. A virtual reality experience that people can access on their phones and laptops settled $2.5 trillion worth of transactions (which in the real world is equivalent to the net worth of VISA transactions) in the *second quarter of one year*. How the fuck did they do this?

Decentraland uses its own currency called mana, which you can obtain through stock. It can appreciate in value significantly and can be used to purchase unique items, called nonfungible tokens (NFTs). NFTs are unique digital representations of assets, real or digital. For example, the future could see a university degree issued as an NFT and linked through online social platforms like LinkedIn. As there's only one of them, the NFT is unique in its digital right. Because each NFT is unique, they are not interchangeable, so members from this digital world are able to buy or sell ownership of certain things through NFTs in the form of artwork,

* www.cnbc.com/2021/05/10/ethereum-eth-price-soars-above-4000-for-the-first-time.html

music and, yes, even land. Republic Realm made news in 2021 for making the largest purchase of NFT land at nearly $1 million, approximately sixteen acres of virtual land*. As long as there are people using this world as a domain for creation, purchases and sales and attracting people, the land will hold value. So, is it any surprise that social media company Facebook announced the launch of its own metaverse in 2021?

Is the future of social media metaverses? Even now, most of us are spending over ten hours on our phones each day without using metaverses. I – like many of you reading this – am ashamed that my daily average screen time on my phone alone is nine hours and ten minutes, since I tell everyone I spend most of my day writing this book on my laptop. Although my mum would strongly disagree.

'Yewande, I've sat here for thirty minutes. You haven't said a word to me; you've just been pressing that phone and taking videos since morning. What kind of addiction is this? Are you the only one to ever use a phone?' she shouted in frustration.

My mum, like many African women, has mastered the fine art of exaggeration. However, there was some truth to her statement. Many of us *are* addicted to our phones and social media. Research from app maker

* https://www.reuters.com/article/us-fintech-nft-land-idCAKCN2DU1GA

Locket shows that the average person checks their phone 110 times per day*. One in five British teenagers spend spend up to five hours daily on social platforms, according to research from the University of Glasgow[†]. While we're using social media, our perception of time is dramatically warped to the point where we underestimate the hours we spend commenting, double tapping, posting and online stalking – yes, stalking! We've all done it, that awkward moment when you recognise someone in public and shockingly remember you only know who they are because you got carried away and discovered they're actually your best friend's brother's ex-girlfriend's cousin's sister. And you landed on their Instagram account last week. But that's beside the point. The point is we are fuelling this addiction despite research showing it may have a negative impact on our wellbeing, according to reports from the BBC.[‡] But we choose to ignite the flame, an addiction that is making social media savvies a lot of money.

When was the last time you bought something because

* https://techland.time.com/2013/10/08/study-says-we-unlock-our-phones-a-lot-each-day
† Scott, H., Biello, S. M., & Woods, H. (2019, February 19). Social media use and adolescent sleep patterns: cross-sectional findings from the UK Millennium Cohort Study. https://doi.org/10.31234/osf.io/z7kpf
‡ 'Sept 21, Is social media bad for your mental health?', *The Week*, https://www.theweek.co.uk/checked-out/90557/is-social-media-bad-for-your-mental-health

of a newspaper or TV ad? Would you say you prefer recommendations from people you know, look up to or admire in some way? If your answer is yes, then that's a dummy's definition of how the influencer market works. From beauty and fashion to fitness influencers, the last decade has witnessed a proliferation of social creators who have transformed the marketing world, encouraging entrepreneurship, engaging in self-branding and subsequently branching out into mainstream cultural industries. The consumer marketing industry has shifted its power dynamic, with consumers demanding real authentic marketing and relatable people to front campaigns. Now more than ever, people are turning to social media personalities for advice and recommendations about products and services. And the numbers don't lie; according to exclusive reports from research company MarketsandMarkets, the influencer marketing industry will be worth $22.3 billion by 2024[*]. I know what you're thinking – that's a lot of zeros, right? And if I'm right, your next question might be, 'Sis, tell us how to get that influencer bag'.

Most of you reading this will know that I'm quite new to the influencing world. Social media was never something that I thought had longevity or could potentially

[*] www.prnewswire.com/news-releases/influencer-marketing-platform-market-worth-22-3-billion-by-2024--exclusive-report-by-marketsand-markets-300878496.htmlmarketsandmarkets-300878496.html

be a full-time job, let alone a business, until 2019. By trade, I would describe myself as a biotechnologist with expertise in upstream and downstream manufacturing of biologics. But my life drastically changed in 2019 when I went on a dating show and came out with nearly a million followers. I had the choice of going back to the field I spent five years training for or diving into this world of social media. Of course, by now it's not a secret what path I decided to pursue. Why did I pick social media? It was a numbers game, really. I wanted some sort of financial freedom, and utilising my platform was an easy way to achieve that. That's me being honest, my unfiltered truth. I could see the endless possibilities of building a career on social media. Working with brands I was passionate about and also building a brand for myself and making a name in the industry, and possibly owning a business or two in the future. I mean, it's 2022 and here I am publishing this book.

Unfortunately, I don't have the secret formula to what makes the right kind of influencer but, being honest, I don't think anyone does. But I have learnt a few things along the way. The first one is authenticity: no one likes an insincere bitch, and not only that, it also builds distrust with any audience. Imagine me trying to sell you a miracle serum that 'clears hyperpigmentation overnight with just one pump – swipe up #ad'. If it didn't work (and it wouldn't), you'd unfollow me out of disgust and utter second-hand embarrassment. To be fair, I'd be offended if you didn't because that is just criminal. Secondly, for creating high quality content (something I'm still working on) it's important to invest in good quality equipment and be meticulous and intentional with outfit styling – branding is everything. Third, community development: building a community of people who trust you by interacting with them on social media platforms and also privately in messages. So, when you see some influencers participate in question boxes with a caption 'Let's catch up' or 'I miss you guys', it's because interaction is key and helps build strong relationships with followers. Yes, having millions of followers is great, but if no one interacts with your content, what happens then? No brand deals, sis. Fourth is trust. Would you buy a product off someone you thought was sketchy? The answer is NO, so why would you buy a product on Instagram if you didn't trust the person promoting it? Lastly, passion. Authenticity is the glue that creates a bridge between influencers and audiences and passion is the fuel. And much like authenticity, passion can't be faked. Imagine someone trying to sell you whitening teeth strips in a monosyllabic tone? It's a no from me, sis.

I guess these steps sound easy; some could call it a dummy's guide to influencing. But where there's a system, there's a flaw. And this particular flaw is the systemic racism that is built into the influencer culture and the product. Well, that's pay disparities. Along with unfavourable algorithmic bias created by engineers, biases that in my opinion are detrimental to the success or failure of Black creators. Don't get me wrong, of course racial pay gaps are an issue across all industries but due to the lack of regulation governing this industry, it is quickly swept under the carpet.

Last year taught me that no matter how many followers you have or what your engagement rate is, if you weren't white, you just weren't 'THAT GIRL' to a lot of brands.

'Ahh, babe, congrats on your collab. You smashed it,' I congratulated Emily. Although we weren't close, I was happy for her. I think a small part of me was congratulating her on surviving a brand deal with a company we both worked for. A brand that was notorious in the industry for their vile treatment of influencers.

'Thanks babe. Honestly never going to work with them again. So glad my contract is over. He's a proper cunt, he is,' she voiced in the most resentful and frustrated tone, wearing a look of pure unfiltered rage I had never seen before.

'Babe, you don't mind if I ask you how much you got paid for your collab?' she asked curiously.

I paused for a minute before I responded. I knew it was important for me to be transparent about my pay in order to bridge the gap, but I somehow knew that even with Emily fewer less than half my followers and similar engagement rates, she would have still taken a bigger cheque home; after all she had the 'look' they all wanted. So, I added an extra couple of thousands to the figure and replied to her in a tone that translated my disgust. The corners of her eyes creased with concern as she looked at me with cautious evaluation.

'WHAT! That's crazy. Honestly babe, they pay so shit,' she rambled on before telling me she was paid twice as much as me! Even with my lie! But I wondered if like me she altered this figure, but in her case played it down. I acted surprised and bewildered, entertaining the atmosphere in the room. I zoomed out, deep in thought, while the girls chatted among themselves. What I failed to tell Emily was after I signed the contract with them, they also requested I pay for the shoot location for the campaign, because they had run out of budget. Of course, I refused and called them out on their bullshit, only for them to tell me they made an error, and the message wasn't directed at me. OKAY, KAREN. A company worth over a hundred million pounds ran out of budget without incorporating costs for the shoot location. If that doesn't scream anti–Black, I don't know what does.

Some people reading this might think, 'well, go get a real job and maybe you might not be faced with these issues. You get paid loads anyways.' My response? Suck your mum! This is an issue of systemic injustice that has been ignored for far too long. It's unfair that a factor such as race can severely hinder a person's financial progression and their ability to monetise their content while their white counterparts succeed. Forcing Black creators to work twice as hard for half the reward. How do we combat this? Transparency and challenging systemic racism. An Instagram page I came across a couple of months ago that is helping to combat this issue is @influencerpaygap. Dedicated to transparency and accountability in the industry, it showcases factors like following count, engagement rate, race and how much influencers are offered for partnerships in order to encourage equity. Of course, we have a long way to go in rectifying these disparities but it's indisputable that efforts like these go a long way in dismantling racial inequalities within the influencer market.

Social media can act as an alternative universe, a brisk escape from reality where people come together to talk about the mundane aspects of everyday life. We are double tapping pictures of Instagram baddies but for some it also serves as a platform for their voices to be heard. A platform where injustices can be brought to light. We live in an age where a simple poignant message from an account with sixty followers can be shared on Twitter and, within twenty-four hours, attract a huge amount of traffic, with thousands and thousands of retweets, likes and shares. Social media enables people to keep up with issues in real time across the globe. Sharing the same message within minutes.

A pivotal moment in Black history was the murder of George Floyd, which was witnessed by billions of people across the world in real time, allowing people to engage in ways that weren't possible twenty years ago. Millennials and Gen Z have changed the game with digital activism and debunking the notion that digital action can't make a difference. Although those foundations were set by those in the Gen X, Millennials and Gen Z have challenged and changed these precedents by bringing these demonstrations to a place that feels familiar – the digital era, social media. Telling their friends to #PullUp and call out racial injustices and a list of other issues including, but obviously not limited to, gun control, domestic abuse and climate change. Sparking the second wave of the #BlackLivesMatter movement in June 2020 was a simple hashtag that turned into a cry for change. A movement that I took part in, marching on the streets of London, using our voices to command for justice. There was something so special about being part of that historical moment. What felt like beautiful chaos, I couldn't help but stand still and take in a moment where we were not only social media savvies, we were all also activists in our own right. I paused and watched as thousands of people marched through the streets of London with conviction and anguish in their voices. I watched how fast this message travelled all while everything still felt very still. People took out their smartphones and captured videos and images to post on all their social media platforms. I watched how fast the images travelled and how they were received with love, pain and gratitude. It wasn't long until these messages were integrated into sports and politics. Videos emerged of people taking the knee in solidarity and allyship. It was an unspeakably tragic moment, but it was a moment that was captured and, through the power of social media, we were able to get some sort of justice for George's family, all the while campaigning for change throughout the globe and tackling institutional and systemic racism.

With the evolution of social media, it became evident that many government officials who were operating in a dictatorship under the illusion of a democracy were frightened once they got a whiff of the power social media had in challenging their power dynamics and making real change.

'AAYY! Did you see Twitter deleted Buhari's tweet yesterday? Fire on the mountain oo!' My sister came charging into my room with both hands on her head, ready to sit down and gist about the aftermath that was due to come. The day before Muhammadu Buhari, President of Nigeria, released a statement through a tweet in response to the digital protest #ENDSARS, a hashtag that led to an international outcry about police brutality and the corruption within the police force in Nigeria.

He tweeted, 'Many of those misbehaving today are too young to be aware of the destruction and loss of lives that occurred during the Nigerian Civil War, those of us in the fields for thirty months, who went through the war, will treat them in the language they understand.' This was a direct reference to the 1967 Nigerian Civil War where over a million people were brutally killed*. Of course, this disgusting tweet was deleted as it violated the app's regulation against abusive behaviour. If you ask me for my opinion, I'd say his efforts at stopping the protest were failing and he was embarrassed. Instead of listening to what the people had to say and aligning correct governance to rectify the issue, his response was to ban Twitter, consequently dismissing and taking away freedom of speech from many young Nigerians, and prosecuting anyone who didn't comply. My biggest fear is that social media moves too fast, allowing some things and decisions like this not to even feel real. Because of the speed at which things move on digital platforms, they easily fall through the cracks, allowing for a new bigger

* https://www.aljazeera.com/features/2020/1/15/nigerians-mark-50-years-of-end-of-bloody-civil-war

story to emerge. It almost feels like some type of alternative universe in which things just keep spinning.

Social media does a great job of creating an optical illusion of reality, or maybe we create this ourselves, by posting a reality we want people to see. I mean who wants to post a video of themselves sobbing with the soundtrack of *All My Friends Are Dead* on social media with the caption, 'I feel lost confused and on the edge of a mental breakdown. Hope you guys have a fab day though #BetterDays #PrayForMe'? Yeah, I wouldn't hold my breath. I've always been able to differentiate between social media and real life. Although on some occasions I find myself deep on my 'explore' page wondering why I don't have a millionaire boyfriend who wants to shower me with gifts and fly me away for date nights in Turks and Caicos. But somehow, I seem to always shake myself back into reality and remind myself that even though a picture might tell a thousand words, those words are none of my business. However, I found myself contributing to this issue by creating warped realities, allowing viewers to buy into a perception of a world that I created, one that was false, indirectly altering our collective sense of reality outside of the digital world. I think by now it's fair to say most of us are aware that social media – and especially Instagram – is not a real place.

As I write this, I vividly remember posting a picture on Instagram with a practised smile and a caption starting with 'So happy . . .' while having one of the saddest and darkest weeks of my life. I had created a pristine profile full of images, videos and stories of me with my glam team, flying out for work and signing exclusive deals! But I was working so hard because I was scared to stop. I felt like I had to make people believe I was living the dream, imitating pictures and videos I had seen on my explore page as #goals when in actual fact the more I tried to emulate those images, the more unhappy it made me.

'Okay, so Yewande, press shots. I want big smiles, I want jumps, have fun, unleash that inner DIVA, GO!' Henry the shoot coordinator yelled across the set enthusiastically while looking at the images on the output monitor.

It was in that very moment that I cracked. I realised I had been smiling so much for pictures and videos that I'd lost myself in that very same smile. It had become a reflex as a pose to a response to a stimulus. When I smiled, I couldn't tell what emotion I felt in that moment. It was just something I did upon action and the worst thing was I carried on, like it was normal. I continued posting images as if my entire reality was in perpetual bliss because I had total jurisdiction over the content I posted. And besides, I was a slave to the algorithm. I couldn't just stop. After weeks of desperately trying to figure out what pleased the powers that be, how could I just stop? But I could, I could stop. All I needed to do was STOP. Here I was prioritising a computerised system over my wellbeing. A system made by software engineers who probably haven't showered today. A mistake I made was not being able to recognise the damage I was doing and the unrealistic expectations I had set for myself and others who were consuming my content.

Another mistake I made was underestimating the gravity of gossip forums and their ability to spread news faster than Covid in a large crowd. My miscalculation was quickly corrected in November 2019 when I found myself the subject of a series of Instagram blogs. They accused me of three things: taking cocaine, being aware that another person was on drugs and being deviously calculated enough to expose them on my Instagram story out of jealousy and resentment.

Being thrown into the limelight is something you think you can prepare yourself and handle. Some extra thousand followers, a brand deal or two, a couple of extra zeros in your bank account and maybe a couple of bum bitches hating on you, but that was all fine because the pros far outweighed the cons. All things I convinced myself I could handle, an equation I just had to crack. But nothing can ever set you up for the dramatic shift you have to quickly adapt to, especially with over-night fame. And no, I don't say this to look for your sympathy or empathy because 'anonhater123', one of my favourite troll accounts, has repeatedly told me and everyone like me who is trying to make a living on social media to simply fuck off. *'They literally went on a TV show to get millions of followers. They asked for it, it comes with the job, get over it.'*

Being involved in a social media scandal with mainstream media outlets picking up the story and running with their own narrative chokes you with a wash of anxiety and rage that is too painful to put into words. Each new story with falsified updates from 'close sources' shakes you with paranoia. A day that still churns my stomach and leaves me feeling nauseated when I'm reminded about it was a day I was supposed to spend celebrating a close friend.

'Babe, don't be late, press gets there at ten . . . can you bring some lash glue with you please? These are already coming off and DON'T BE FUCKING LATE' – a message I read aloud while spinning around my room dusting off my retired dance moves for the session that was about to commence. I'd promised myself I was going to get loose, have a great bloody time and get absolutely hammered. I grabbed whatever coat was closest and stomped down the stairs in heels, running awkwardly into my Addison Lee that I had kept waiting an extra twenty minutes because I couldn't decide whether the trousers or the skirt gave me the illusion of a bigger bum. As I got out of the car, I was blinded by a swarm of paparazzi who had been tasked with capturing images of all the celebs and influencers who walked the carpet before entering the event.

'YEWANDE! Did you bring the glue?' Michelle shouted, her voice tight with panic, oblivious to the fact she had ruined at least five press shots of girls on the carpet. I shoved my hand down my bra and pulled out a small tube of glue. She grabbed me by the wrist and dragged me into the venue and straight to the bathroom.

'So, who do you have your eye on tonight, then?' she smirked into the mirror, her reflection looking directly at me as she painted her lash strip with glue.

'No one, we literally just got in.' I blushed.

'Bitch, you asked Tatianna to send you the guestlist on the group chat, so I know you're lying,' she demanded.

'Okay, soo, you know Sam . . .' I teased while avoiding eye contact.

'Shut the front door. You need some action! I'm going to be your wing woman,' she squealed, jumping up and down while the other girls in the bathroom gave her embarrassed and confused stares.

We gallivanted round the venue taking pictures and picking up the strongest drink the bartender had to offer with each lap. We danced in deep euphoria, and I tested out the strength of my knees reciting famous words from Saweetie's 'My Type' before we were kicked out of the venue at 1 a.m. However, I still hadn't been able to make a move on Sam. I mean, we exchanged a few words, but that was it. We all decided that night was too early to end so we ran into whatever black taxi was available and made our way to Cirque. While in the taxi, I realised I was having such a good night that I hadn't updated my followers about what I was doing and where I was. I could hear my manager's voice in my ears telling me that I needed to be more active on social media and in real time. My audience needed to get a front row seat into my life. That's what social media's all about, you see. People need to buy into you, they need to be invested and follow your journey. The ups and the downs, making yourself feel more 'real' and accessible. So, I reposted some of the videos I was tagged in, with the intention of getting more organic content when we arrived. When we got in, I drank any drink that was handed my way – by then, I was so intoxicated I couldn't even taste the alcohol. I opened Instagram and posted a myriad of stories throughout the night to show people how much fun we were having, how lit our section was and ultim-ately behind the scenes of influencers gone wild. I put my phone away and spent most of the night running away from people with camera phones and snogging Sam in whatever area was closed off to the public. We both agreed we didn't want our business to be plastered on the front page of the *Daily Mail* in the morning. I somehow woke up the next morning in last night's clothes and shoes with gaps in my memory. I had no recollection of how I got home and to this day I'm unable to fill in the blanks. I tried to trace my steps by watching my own Instagram story on replay and that's when I saw a really bad clip of Tatianna, who looked as bad as I felt. I quickly deleted the story regardless of the fact it had been viewed by hundreds of thousands of people. I slept off as much of my hangover I could before I was woken up with calls and texts that I was trending on Twitter and all over Instagram.

'Don't say anything, don't post anything. Even if you did or didn't do it, keep your head down,' was the advice from my manager, rattled off with brisk authority, leaving no room for me to comment before telling me she was on it and hanging up abruptly. I opened Twitter and it wasn't long till I was suffocated with speculation and judgement with every tweet, retweet and like.

Tweets, comments and messages multiplied by the minute. Instagram DMs from strangers telling me to kill myself because I had ruined Tatianna's career before it had even begun. I became obsessed with reading everything. With each message a great sense of weariness swept over me, sucking my energy and slowly draining me both mentally and physically.

'I thought highly of you, but you're a real snake in the green grass.' 'How could you do such an evil thing to Tatianna. You're a vile human being. Full stop!' 'One minute of fame and they're off their heads on coke!' were some of the messages that flooded my social media. I felt layers of unsettling emotion. I watched my eyes widen and rim with tears on the screen of my phone and a slow fury began to consume me. Tatianna and I had spent the whole day together, both high on life and intoxicated with alcohol. No drugs were ever involved. I've never taken or been offered drugs in my entire life, so how the fuck was I here? I was advised against making a statement, because I couldn't confirm that there were no drugs at the event and if this was to come out, I would be discredited regardless of the fact that we were not involved. The scandal went on for days, but it felt like weeks. My ears could hear every tweet that was posted, whispers of people in the streets and eyes that revealed their internal monologue. Above all, I feared how one snap I posted on social media could affect a friendship that was already shaky. How one snap, coupled with powerful influence on social media, could potentially affect both of our careers, discredit our names and brands that were barely established. All from one user on the internet reposting a video with an inaccurate caption. Moral of the story? Be careful with what you share on social media, there are some things you just can't take back.

A lot of people ask where Gen Z and Millennials who chose social media as their primary source of income are going to be in twenty years, with the influx of young adults choosing a career in social media instead of other traditional forms of work in the healthcare, legal, IT and other sectors. To me, the answer is simple: they'll be in marketing. Executives, creative directors of brands worth millions of dollars and ultimately CEOs of their own businesses. A big trend I've noticed is influencers rebranding into business owners. While not every influencer might have entrepreneurial flair, many do and are seeing gaps in the market they can fill with a product or service. Backed by an army of loyal followers and a creditable brand they've built for years, influencers are able to take the skills they've learnt on digital platforms and incorporate them into their own marketing campaigns, combining authenticity and a great product. Having an audience that already buys into your recommendations makes it easier to sell a product from your own business due to the engagement, a sense of connectedness and the interpersonal relationship your audience has with you already. With the right team in place there's no reason these businesses can't be worth billions in twenty years. Just look at Kylie Jenner, an influencer extraordinaire who built her brand's empire on social media and is currently worth hundreds of millions of dollars, although is not yet a billionaire, as previously claimed by experts[*].

---

[*] hwww.forbes.com/video/6160187082001/why-kylie-jenner-is-no-longer-a-billionaire/?sh=7162b6055ae0

Many of you who are holding this book either bought it because you've built some emotional attachment to me through watching my journey and wanted to support your good sis (thank you!) or you swiped up on one of the links I've added to many of my social posts. Some may argue that in the future social media won't be as powerful as it is today, but I disagree. Social media isn't going anywhere and that's just a new reality we have to contend with. The question is, is there a balance? And how do we find it? Living in a digital age allows us to stay well connected with friends and family and keeps us informed about what's going on around the world in real time. Social media has given us the tools and the voice to establish real change; it's given a voice to the marginalised voices, and it's been liberating, especially for those who have been silenced by gerontocracy. Although there are many positive sides to social media, it would be naïve to just focus on this and not to touch on the damaging consequences it's had for our mental health, perceived realities and physical wellbeing. Constant pressure to keep up with appearances will only lead to unhappiness and dissatisfaction, but I do believe there's a balance and that's remembering the importance of real-life interaction, being cautious about the type of images and messages you ingest. Created realities are not enough to have you evaluating your entire existence over a tub of ice cream in the dark!

The idea that you have to create a polished version of yourself on social media is ludicrous and very hard to maintain. There's no such thing as a perfect picture so never compare yourself or your life to anyone else's. That being said it's only natural that I ask myself what I intend to do with the platform I have, and in what direction I see it taking me. A typical answer from an influencer would be, 'I want to use my platform to make real change and talk about important topics within the community'. Of course their intentions sound benevolent and altruistic. However, the reality is, they aren't. Yes, I said what I said. Most beauty, lifestyle and fashion influencers don't care about worldwide issues, and the fact that we have less than eight years to reverse the effects of global warming before we hit a tipping point of no return. The reality is, as much as you want people to care, they just don't give a fuck. Not everyone has the ability and the skill set to be an activist, and they shouldn't feel the need to. You don't follow them for that; you follow them because you want to be updated on the latest fashion trends, you like how they make their avocado on toast or you want to learn how to make your face structurally symmetric using Fenty's new skin concealers. So, my truth is I want to use my platform to create a life for myself that I've always dreamt of. I didn't have much growing up, so being financially stable is something that has always been very important to me. The goal was never to be an influencer forever; the toxic side of the internet is something I cannot contend with for the rest of my career. I see myself as a business owner, using the marketing tools I've learnt from social media and the platform I have to make this happen. But of course, it's not all about securing the bag, it's also about having purpose while remaining true to yourself. That's why you're holding this book. Yes, I was paid to write it, but like many published authors, I could have taken a back seat and published with a ghost writer and stuck a very fancy picture of myself smiling on the cover. But I wanted to pour back into you, the same way you filled me these past few years. I wanted to leave you with something that I hope changes you positively in some way. I want my impact to be purposeful, deliberate and genuine.

Chapter Seven: Heaven Help Me

'Now, now, you'll need to go to confession and say at least two hail Marys for that lie' – Confessions of a Nigerian church girl

Trigger warning: domestic abuse

If you read the contents page before landing on this chapter, I'm pretty sure you would have been a little confused about why it made the final cut of the book. Now, I'm not a religious person, and I've always had an unusual relationship with it, but I'm going to talk about dating in the next chapter and this should contextualise it a ~~bit~~ lot. My family are Christians but most of my beliefs came from being raised in a Catholic school and a predominantly Catholic country, Ireland.

We won't get into too much politics about how Catholicism came about, but just know we don't celebrate St Paddy's Day for nothing. I was in a mixed school until the age of seven, when the boys left and went to the school across the road to be taught by the Christian

Brothers. I'd never stepped foot into that school but there were rumours that they got preferential treatment. The only time we saw them was in Mass for preparation for our First Holy Communion and then for Confirmation a couple of years after. I never read much into our separation, but now looking back, I can make sense of it. Seven was around the age boys in my class didn't seem so gross to the girls. So, it was to prevent sin, a lustful eye. Seven was the age where the Catholic Church determined you to be 'of reason', being able to determine right from wrong. What ended up happening was the same boys we grew up with from the age of four till the age of seven had me and my pre-teen classmates giggling and whispering about which one was the cutest in the back of Mass – and believe me, I can already see the irony. Before long, it was time for me to tell Father O'Neil all the unholy thoughts I had been having about Jerry.

Mrs Keogh's favourite religious holiday was Easter. Many would think it was because we were celebrating the rebirth of our Lord and saviour, Jesus Christ, but they would've been wrong. It was mainly because Ash Wednesday was a few weeks before Easter and it wasn't uncommon for people to keep the commitments they made for Lent for the rest of the year. Lord knows, Mrs Keogh would have dragged me by the hair and placed me in front of Father O'Neil herself if I showed up to school late that day. You see, every year she made me promise I'd give up lateness for the six weeks of Lent and prayed I'd keep it up throughout the year. I guess God never quite got round to answering her prayer.

Throughout most of my adolescent life, I practised two faiths. I spent some Sundays in Mass, pampering my knees on the kneeler and smiling about how they were afforded the grace of comfort; and other Sundays, I was in Pentecostal church with ashy knees from the cold hard surface I knelt on while praying for forgiveness of sin in Sista Ronke's Bible Study class as she told us we were all bound to burn in hell for eternity for our sins of fornication, lying and stealing. Like many Christians, I believe that there is only one true God, and he gave up his only begotten son as an act of redemption. To simply believe in him is to be saved from eternal damnation. I know, harsh ending, but a very true and real belief. My experiences with life coupled with socially constructed 'norms' and a choice in university education that was hell bent on teaching me about the inconclusive dogmas on the evolution of life have naturally shaped a new perspective on how I look at religion. I found myself asking more questions and being more open-minded, despite what I was learning early on in Sunday School, that it's a sin to question God. *'Blasphemy! Don't even think about it'* was the response to any question that started with *'how . . .'* and so naturally, I became even more curious. Although my questions remained unanswered and were met with hostility and even disgust, I grew inquisitive. I found myself always coming back to the word religion. Religion. What *is* religion? From a simplistic viewpoint, many would say it is a social-cultural system where different beliefs and practices are adopted. But for me, religion now serves as a socially constructed term used to place people in boxes, keep them bound and excuse them from immoral acts, a tool sometimes used by fundamentalists and narcissists.

Most of the women in the congregation treated Sunday's church services as group therapy sessions. Well, they were respectful enough to wait till after the service was over before freely giving opinions on issues that were none of their concern. Gossip about whose marriage was failing, whether Deacon Psalm had been altering the financial books and pocketing what he could to buy himself a new car. The biggest mystery of all was which choir member(s) had fallen captive to the choir master's wandering eye and indulged in extramarital affairs. Of course, my eyes were like silver lightning, sharp enough to catch a smile that lingered too long, fingers that hovered over body parts that should've been left alone and, of course, the constant urge to always remain connected through intense sessions of unbreakable eye contact.

'I wanted to stay quiet, but as soon as you sat beside

me, I felt the Holy Spirit move me to tell you how Sista Margaret wants to disgrace us women in the church,' I heard Sista Rose whisper while rubbing shoulders mischievously with Sista Julie.

'You have come again. What have you heard this time?' Sista Julie laughed to herself with an eager ear to hear the answer.

'Deacon Psalm is cheating on his wife *AGAIN*.' She paused and clapped her hands loudly to emphasise her disgust. 'This time it is Sista Ronke that has fallen into his trap!' she exclaimed with a hint of disappointment.

The news didn't come to a surprise to either of them, nor did it me; the deacon was an attractive man who didn't believe a word of the sermons he was preaching, nor did he have any respect for the commandments in the Bible. He hid behind his charm and faith, but I had witnessed the ugly truth of his abuse towards his wife and his inability to keep his pants zipped up. As a child I saw him violently push, shove and strangle her until the capillaries in her eyes ruptured. When they were in public, he would substitute his physical abuse with emotional abuse. I could see the indescribable agony in her eyes as each word tore through her. What took me by surprise the most was the response she was met with, in a moment that required strength and love. *'Don't give up, keep praying for him. The Bible says wives, submit your-selves unto your own husbands . . . for the husband is the head of the wife, even as Christ is the head of the Church.'* One woman said. *'All you can do is pray God will change him.'* They all recited this like it was a mantra, the words filled with both pity and judgement somehow. I don't think any of them really believed what they were saying; it was just the best scripture to quote at that moment. It was the moment I truly understand the oppression of women in the Church. I felt so weak and powerless and wasn't intellectually competent enough to put my feelings into words, at least not words that would impact her in a positive way. So, I left them to it and made my way upstairs to Bible Study class.

I was early but I convinced myself that if I arranged the chairs, it would help in my defence when explaining to Sista Ronke about how I forgot to memorise the Bible verse I had been tasked with last week. Before I got to the door, I heard heavy breathing. The closer I got the louder the moans became. They couldn't see me peeking, but I saw him hover over her as she lay on the same table where she had placed spare Bibles for class. As I watched them in their sinful act, I realised this was it, this was the thing Sista Ronke had told us to abstain from until marriage: sex. They were having sex. *She* was having sex with another woman's husband – in church! The realisation made me scream and then quickly clamp my hand over my mouth, but it was too late. They had already seen me peeking through the small gap in the door. Out of shock, Deacon Psalm had let his trousers fall and I could see his bare ass. They covered what shame they could, and the silent tension between us grew until it thickened the air. When the shock wore off, I took my tiny legs, placed each foot in front of the other and attempted to run away as quickly as possible. It wasn't long till Deacon Psalm caught up with me and warned me not to say a word. I knew not to ask questions and decided to stay out of it entirely. I ran downstairs and asked one of the ushers to seat me in the congregation.

Pastor Jacob led the sermon on faith and Christianity with Deacon Psalm by his right-hand side. It baffled me how these esteemed members of the church I once identified with so strongly appeared to have abandoned all their principles, faith and morality on the inside but still appeared as pure conservative Christians on the outside. From an early age, I had subconsciously blurred the lines between prominent figures in religious institutions and God. I truly believed I wasn't holy or deserving enough to have a direct channel of communication with God. I held them to the highest standards, so when I witnessed their sins, I found it hard to make the distinction between religion and faith as separate entities. These figures listed out the requirements needed to be born again and to enter the gates of heaven, pleading with people to forget sin and repent. The hypocrisy enraged me but the guilt of judging them consumed me like water added to an already vigorous fire. Surely, I was just as bad as they were? I couldn't help but fantasise about what type of Christian I wanted to be but felt guilty because it was one that didn't align with what I had been taught. It was one that believed in the pillars of Christianity but questioned a lot of the scriptures in it. One that didn't see everything as black and white, one that no longer believed in religion or the Church but still believed in salvation. Subconsciously, over the years I started deconstructing my faith, trying to identify which of the beliefs I was taught were harmful and which were good and righteous. What I was petrified to say out loud was that I didn't believe in biblical inerrancy, I didn't agree with some of the teaching, I didn't agree with the outdated patriarchal governance of the Church and how it was run.

So, when someone would ask about my faith, I would reply to them with 'I'm Christian, but I'm not religious' almost as if I was apologetic for all the negative connotations that came with being 'religious'. Emphasising the fact that although I had adopted a certain theology, I had chosen aspects to retain based on personal preference. I wanted them to know I had adopted views from palatable unbelievers about gender, sexuality and hell, basically issues not embraced by popular culture. Constantly torn about what a true Christian was supposed to be, an endless circular reasoning that was self-defeating. Looking to scriptures for guidance but constantly feeling deflated when I began to question the words on the page. It took me a while to welcome the idea that I didn't have to choose between believing that the Bible was wholly accurate and that there was flexibility in interpretations of it. It wasn't one or the other. This is something that I've struggled with; it's something that I'm still struggling with. It's just not fair, the words are too old, it's too difficult to tell exactly what's going on or what it is trying to teach you or even how you apply it to your own life. I find myself asking what these words mean to me over three thousand years after they were written.

There's always been this dualistic idea when it comes to the desexualisation and the hypersexualisation of women in Christianity. Where women are either seen as pure and untainted or devious and sexually immoral. Women are consistently told to dress appropriately in order to avoid sexual thoughts and lustful eyes, with no repercussions for the eyes that are sexualising and objectifying them. They are judged by how others perceive them and not by how they behave. For example, the modesty and purity doctrine are still about the objectification of women's bodies. Sexually shaming women and girls based on their sexual freedom and expression. Women are taught that it is their responsibility to dress modestly to avoid lustful eyes and sinful thoughts. Not to say that young boys and men are not included in these conversations but it's an indisputable fact that young girls and women are held to more exacting standards. For years, I grew up with an unhealthy relationship with sex and idolised purity and virtuousness above all, because I believed it would make me holier and more desirable for marriage. This is not to say that I don't agree with people's decision to abstain from sex, practise celibacy or wait to till marriage to have sex, as long as these decisions are made by them, without any institutional bias, shame or fear. I listened to the dogmatic ideologies that were preached about sexuality and gender and became closed-minded to the latter in my early years.

'Gender is fixed, God does not make mistakes, the only relationship that should exist is between a man and a woman, anything else is not of God' were some of the teachings preached in Church with the contradictory statement at the end of the sermon telling us to love our neighbours unconditionally and free from judgement, in the same way God loves us.

I watched how Pastor Jacob called out a man in the middle of service to receive the Holy Spirit that would free him from a life of sexual sin and the 'evil spirit of homosexuality' that had occupied his body. Pastor Jacob never shied away from outbreaks of madness every Sunday. One Sunday, he kept us captive in church for three hours after the sermon had ended because the

Holy Spirit had sent a message that there was a witch in the church. One night during vigil, he cast the spirit of Mami Wata (mermaid) out of a young woman who lived by the river. But nothing made me more uncomfortable than watching him cast what he described as the demon of homosexuality out of a friend I had made in church at the age of thirteen. We were both silenced by fear; I felt guilt at being complicit in such an immoral act. This is the experience that unequivocally changed my outlook on the Church and religion forever.

As simplistic as it may sound, I've adopted a general belief system, for people to build a relationship with God whoever He might be to them, or how they see Him, as opposed to grouping people by religion. It's unfair to think that someone might be condemned to eternal damnation because they were born into what some people might see as the 'wrong religion' and taught the 'wrong' theology about the evolution of life, dismissing the fact they lived a life that was indirectly described as 'Christ-like'. So instead of looking at scriptures with surface-level meanings, I now look at them with a hermeneutical approach, putting aside my systemic bias from what I learnt in church and trusting the relationship I have with God.

I'm not trying to argue that religion itself is fiction. Rather, I'm welcoming the idea that all truth has the structure of some type of fiction. It's a known fact that

167

the Bible was originally written in Hebrew before it was translated to Latin and later into over 700 languages. The tricky thing about direct language translation is that sometimes it misses the essence of the message. I believe it loses its richness and authenticity. Although the Bible is a holy book, I also like to look at it as an anthology, where some writers have been credited for their work and some remain anonymous. Although these books were written with divine intervention from the Holy Spirit, I can't help but question potential human bias in the writing of these scriptures. And for the Old Testament, well it's still unknown who wrote the majority of those books. Words that we hold so dear and are determined as the book of law for Christians. It is not my intention to have a philosophical debate here to determine the existence of a higher being, so please excuse my tone while I find the right words to use.

Some might say deconstructing or challenging the Bible or scriptures within it is done with a subjective interpretation of the passage. Something only done by doubters who no longer believe or are on their way to atheism. But to me, deconstructing is not about demanding answers, because no one among us is all-knowing. It's about giving people the permission to be comfortable to ask questions even though they might not get the answers they're looking for or an answer at all. I'm a scientist, so the question I had to ask myself was whether

I was reading scripture with a hermeneutical approach or with confirmation bias. Plainly, was I reading looking for a deeper meaning or was I looking for information in the Bible that would support my existing beliefs and values? The moment I answered that determined my faith. Without this mindset you're not doing anyone any favours, because then you only have faith through proxy.

When I have told people that I'm deconstructing my faith, all they seem to hear is someone who, in my case, is leaving Christianity, leaving the Church and becoming a non-believer. However, deconstruction is not the end goal; it's a phase you move through to determine your faith. There's no one-size-fits-all paradigm on how or when to deconstruct. Deconstruction is usually triggered by many internal and external factors. For me, one of my main external factors was the Church as an institution and my broken trust in the spiritual leaders within it. At an internal level, I had a wounded heart from the corruption and distrust within the Church. My deconstruction journey started years ago, without me even knowing what the term meant. I deconstructed my religion, but I didn't walk away from my faith in God. I made a transition from mainline Christianity to universalism, to spiritualism, to something without a label at all. But what exactly does that mean for me?

At a high level, it means I focus on the unconditional love God has for all his creations and a belief in salvation of all souls and in Jesus Christ as the son of God. I unlearnt and relearnt who God is to me. But there's still so much I'm learning and figuring out. I don't have all the answers, and I doubt that I or anyone ever will. There are a lot of opinions and ideologies that I have now which will probably be very different in the next five years. And I can't wait to find out what my stance will be then. If we aren't changing, then we aren't evolving and if we aren't evolving then we aren't living.

Chapter Eight: Swipe Left, Swipe Right

'Roses are red, violets are blue. I'm choosing myself; I hope you do too.'

As I sit down to write, I find myself gazing up at my blinding spotlights, watching each light create a memorable prism of colours. In the background, I can hear the echoing noises of *Sex and the City* re-runs on TV – I think Carrie is telling the girls she is leaving Big for the hundredth time. I can just about make out each voice slowly drifting through the abyss of my mind, which is completely blank. It would be peaceful if I hadn't spent hours in this one position trying and failing to figure out how to start this paragraph. I want to talk about dating, love and everything in between. I know what I want to say but my hands remain frozen on my keyboard. Then it hits me – the sad, painful, but very true reality that most of us don't like to admit: we don't know how to date. I can already feel the heavy eye rolls and defensive huffing and puffing. I know you're thinking I should speak for myself, and so I will, but if we are being honest, sis, I'm probably speaking a bit for you too.

Hey, my name is Yewande, and I don't know how to date. How and when did I come to this realisation? Let me take you back to the beginning . . . I grew up with two Nigerian parents, so Western dating was a very foreign concept. *'What do you need a boyfriend for? Read your books!' 'Wait till you're in university. You're too young to be dating!'* were the only replies to my very enthusiastic question of *'can I have a boyfriend?'* Like most first-born Nigerian children, I was somewhat obedient (of course, I had my little rendez-vous here and there with Peter at the back of the school's boiler room, but let's not get into that).

When I was finally old enough to date in my parents' eyes, I lacked a lot of emotional intelligence – something a lot of my peers had learnt throughout the years, while I waited until university. When I started dating, I found it difficult and hostile mainly because I suffer from something I like to call the 'Disney Complex Syndrome' (or DCS for short). Now, I know all my hypochondriacs reading this are getting a little bit too excited and have concluded that without a doubt they suffer from this *very* real syndrome. So, what exactly is DCS?

Growing up in a Black household, one that wasn't affectionate in the slightest, I was conflicted about what love was supposed to look like. I knew what it felt like and when it was authentic and rich in its embrace, but I didn't know how to express it. Almost like a puzzle, you couldn't work out how to finish but knew vaguely where the pieces were supposed to go. Although my parents have been together for over twenty-five years and it is evident that there is love between them, I still felt like I had no real visual representation of this ideology called 'love'.

From an early age, I was indoctrinated into the idea that true, long-lasting romantic love and commitment were mirror images of relationships in magical fairy tales. The only resources I had were in Greek mythology stories like that of Eros (also known as Cupid) and Psyche. When Cupid came upon Psyche, he was captivated by her beauty. He couldn't bear losing her to another man, so he pricked himself with his own arrow of love so that he would only have eyes for her. I mean if that isn't love, I don't know what is.

Films based on books like *To All the Boys I've Loved Before* tell the typical awkward-girl-meets-popular-boy story where they fall in love, then break up, but without a doubt find their way back to their happily ever after. Both are very real and accurate depictions of love, right? These unrealistic standards that are quite unattainable distorted the way I viewed dating, relationships and love. I completely submerged myself into this princess fairy tale fantasy and subsequently was always frustrated when my expectations of the men I dated were never met. Inevitably, with reality being the bitch that she is, the fairy tale evaporated very quickly.

What I realised was that by having this fantasy mindset of waiting for my knight in shining armour to be my 'hero' and 'saviour' and to 'sweep me off my feet', I encouraged 'benevolent sexism', meaning that I condoned the behaviour of giving men a God complex, believing women should be protected (whether intentionally or not), thus justifying gender inequality and reinforcing this message that women were weak, less than and 'needed protection'. After reading Chimamanda Ngozi Adichie's book *We Should All Be Feminists*, I was determined more than ever to not be a bad feminist, to stop upholding rigid gender roles that were suffocating and straining on my relationships and to allow for more fluidity, creating room for spontaneity, intimacy and fun.

So, the question is: where do we – or at least *I* – go from here? What does love really look like? Shaking off all my preconceptions and unrealistic notions and just allowing it to be and to flow naturally. Does the burning, fiery sensation you feel at the start of a romance really last forever? Or is that just lust? I always assumed that I would have found my long-lost soulmate by now and we'd be somewhere in Turks and Caicos having sex, not just regular sex – *amazing* sex, fifty shades of filth to be exact. Instead, I'm here in bed reflecting on my horrendous dating history while wearing my black silk bonnet, with peppermint and olive oil escaping my scalp and dripping down my forehead, the strong scents suffocating my lungs.

It seems that many of my peers were able to find their soulmates on dating apps like Plenty of Fish, Tinder and Grindr. Unlike them, it was written somewhere in the stars for me to take a more strenuous route. I mean, who the fuck wrote that? I've had my fair share of dating app horror stories, and mentally as a Black woman, it's not the most welcoming space, in my opinion.

'I've never been with a Black woman before.'
'My favourite category to watch is Ebony.'
'So, can you twerk like Megan Thee Stallion?'
'You have the perfect lips for a blow job.'

Ladies and gentlemen, welcome to a Black woman's Tinder messages (well at least mine!). On their own, these messages might evoke an eye roll or tutting, but cumulatively they were enough to make me leave the app altogether. Now I can reminisce about the good ol' days and have joined a more exclusive dating app: Raya. My current total match count consists of 1% Black men, with other ethnicities just sending one-word questions like *'Sex?'* Look at this for growth!

As a young Black woman, I've become very aware of

this hypersexualisation, but it's not a new phenomenon. Let's look at the tragic story of Sara Baartman, a Khoikhoi woman born in 1775 in modern-day South Africa. Baartman was trafficked to Europe to exhibit her body, in particular her buttocks, after signing a contract, although she couldn't read or write the language it was written in. Millions came to see her, not as a person but because of their curious fascination with African people. She was ridiculed, dehumanised and objectified. After she died, her (sexual) organs and bones remained on display in a museum in Paris until 1974. Her remains weren't repatriated and buried until 2002. There are echoes of the animalistic dehumanisation of Black women's bodies still seen today like with Nicki Minaj's wax figure. The wax figure made its European debut at Madame Tussauds in Berlin in January 2020. It was supposed to depict her 2014 music video for 'Anaconda' and is permanently perched on all fours in a black thong, a gold, beaded top, and strappy heels*. While the outfit matches the music video, the figure's face doesn't resemble Minaj's – but more disturbing was the way some people posed with it. Many people pointed out that for all her accomplishments, the choice was made to display

* Adejobi, Alicia, Jan 2020, 'Nicki Minaj's waxwork at Madame Tussauds looks nothing like her and fans are crying', *Metro*, https://metro.co.uk/2020/01/07/nicki-minajs-waxwork-madame-tussauds-looks-nothing-like-fans-crying-12019353

a likeness of Minaj in a vulnerable and sexualised position that, arguably, reduces her to a sexual object rather than an influential and powerful woman who is sexy. There is a very faint argument to be made to explain why the pose was chosen: the video, which her wax figure is portraying, broke a VEVO record and its exclusion from the Video of the Year award nominations at the VMAs highlighted the discrepancy and discrimination for Black women in the industry. However, the blank gaze from her wax figure while visitors simulate sex acts on it is uncomfortably reminiscent of how women, and more specifically Black women, are sexualised – sometimes against their will. If you are in any doubt of the misogynoir, let's compare this to at another wax figure in the same museum: Channing Tatum, star of *Magic Mike*. His figure is stood with hands in its pockets, wearing a suit and tie rather than half-naked and grinding on a pole.

This hypersexualisation of Black bodies is deeply rooted in a problematic ideology at its core, that being that whiteness is the norm; it's pure and virtuous. Meanwhile, Blackness is promiscuous, tainted and exotic. It is propelled by an immoral desire to partake in the fallaciously depicted 'deviancy' of Black sexuality, to explore Black bodies as if these bodies are theirs to conquer. This authority is especially pressing for Black women, who have historically and contemporarily been denied power over their representation. Often these representations are in response to white heteropatriarchal depictions of Black women. These oppressive racial narratives created to subjugate Black people and control their bodies are still prevalent today.

Let's look at three types of stereotypes given to Black women and how they still affect us today: The Mammy, the Jezebel and the Sapphire. Submissive, sexy and sassy. Three stereotypes of Black women that are still perpetuated through the media, repeatedly. The Mammy is familiar to people, often taking care of the family. She is perceived as asexual and aromantic and doesn't have a life of her own. She is only there to support the white family. Famous examples of this are the maids from *The Help*.

The second stereotype is the Jezebel, someone who is generally sexually aggressive, with an intense sexual appetite. Her only power is her body, and this is the extent of the influence she has over men. The role Halle Berry played in *Monster's Ball* is a prime example. Finally, the Sapphire stereotype that's seen on TV more than anything else. She's usually opinionated, sassy, angry, aggressive, a bully and manipulative. If married, you can guarantee she emasculates her husband. A representation of 'the angry Black woman' that's still used today. A brilliant example is Toni from *Girlfriends*.

Throughout history these depictions of Black women have often been used to put forward oppressive ideologies. These ideologies can be seen as by-products of digital sexual racism in online dating derived from historical white supremacist roots. Their effects on Black women attempting to navigate the already murky waters of the swamp scene that is modern dating can be detrimental to the experience.

So, every Tom, Dick and Harry on Tinder, the answer to your question is no. My knees are not as strong as Megan Thee Stallion's, and the fact that you've never been with a Black woman before is a red flag, not a turn-on. Please don't talk to me about how you've sexualised me based on three pictures my friends helped me pick.

So, where does this leave me? Of course, I'm not going to date those who have fetishised me. I'm quick to shut down any conversation containing red flags, fetishisms or outright insults with swiftness. An affirmation I use when it gets too much: *I am a Black woman. I am not aggressive. My body does not exist to satisfy your sexual urges. I am a vessel of love; I am deserving of love, and I have a lot of love to give.*

I am living in a time where the pressure to be married by the age of thirty (twenty-five if you're Nigerian) is unbearable. Last year, I was on the phone with my mother for over an hour as she prayed for me to find my husband before the end of 2021, when I turned twenty-six. The phone call lasted 72 minutes and 16 seconds. A step down from her last record of 120 minutes last month to talk about a dream she had, which was, of course, intertwined with the fact that I was *still* not dating anyone.

'Yewande, I don't want you to get offended, but they'll say I'm not a good mother if I don't ask.'

Despite my mum's apologetic tone, I rolled my eyes and held my breath. I already knew what was coming but her reference to 'they' had my blood silently boiling; why was it anyone's business whether I was dating or not?

'So, you're going to tell me you're not even dating anyone, not even one person?' she asked inquisitively.

'No, I'm not! If I was, I would tell you so you would leave me alone!' I joked.

She yammered on about what she described as an 'unfortunate situation' of a Nigerian woman she knew in her mid-thirties who had bagged herself a science degree, a fantastic job in a biopharmaceutical company, but was still unmarried – an African mum's worst nightmare, but why? Why was there a timestamp sealed and locked on what constitutes a pragmatic age to get married followed sharply by the need to reproduce?

We went back and forth, with her adding, 'Anyways, just remember, we're not like those white people. As long as you don't tell me you don't want to get married, that would be a big problem . . .'

It was the first time I considered what life would look like if I didn't get married. That invitation was never welcomed in my household. So, how do I even know if marriage is for me? I never fell into the category of women who had scrapbooks of their fairy tale wedding, with their perfect dress, ring and fixed seating arrangements that were not up for negotiation. The idea, if I'm being honest, gives me anxiety. I keep those unwanted daydreams locked somewhere in my brain. She ended the call by reiterating the fact that time wasn't on my side and to always keep that in mind.

Society tends to attribute certain achievements to particular stages in a person's life: Graduate by twenty-one, get engaged by twenty-five, be married with kids by twenty-seven and of course, become a homeowner before thirty (when I assume life is supposed to dramatically cease). Yes, you heard that right, ladies and gentlemen, according to Twitter and my mother, life ends at thirty. Keeping those calculations in mind, I'd say I have about five years, give or take. Of course, time is on my side. What even is time? An illusion of foggy memories wrapped up in thoughts of the past and present.

Or was she talking about my biological clock? And if I'm being honest, it's something that I have thought about a lot. I visited a friend of mine who lives in Central London this week and as we gossiped about the most mundane things, we also bonded over shared dating experiences.

'Oh yeah, I froze my eggs the other day,' she blurted

out so casually mid-conversation. Dami has a unique talent for simplifying uncomfortable conversations. With us both being Nigerian, this was definitely a non-traditional and unconventional way of reproducing that would be sure to evoke unwarranted and unsolicited opinions, especially from people in my parents' generation. I could already hear the whispers in the air:

'*A test tube baby?*'

'*Her mum didn't raise her right.*'

'*This is what happens when you bring these children to Europe for better education.*'

'Gwoorrrlll, how was it? You're still so young. What made you decide to do that?' I asked curiously.

She explained the extreme pressure she felt to be married or at least settled into a serious relationship. Unlike me, thirty was right around the corner for her; however, she was not ready to settle for any dick (or Tom or Harry). It was important for her to find love and a genuine lasting connection, no matter how long it took. Dami wanted to do this without constant reminders of the ticking time bomb that was her biological reproduct-ive organs.

'You should look into it. I'll send you the clinic's details,' she suggested in the most welcoming tone.

I picked up my phone to look at the WhatsApp message Dami had just sent. For the first time, I felt like time had truly frozen. I had a choice. I guess, until this point, I'd never stopped to ask myself if I even wanted kids. I still don't have answers to any of these questions and that's okay. I'm just figuring out life one step at a time. When things get too much with dating or looking for a life partner, here's what I've learnt:

- Make a list of what you want in a partner and believe that you are worthy of that.
- Remember that you are enough, especially when the world tries to tell you otherwise.
- There is **nothing** wrong with being unmarried or single at thirty – or at any age.
- Delete the dating apps if they get dry or overwhelming.

'You are gold, don't let anyone treat you like you are silver.' Positive reinforcements like this one from my aunt have stuck with me, especially while dating, where it's so common in our community for Black women to 'date down' or lower their standards, whether this is socio-economically, emotionally or physically. We are all different, so there is no set rule for what makes one person's 'low standard' right or wrong. There are countless debates about the implications of having standards that are deemed too high, but what I continue to ask myself is whether I will be content settling for a relationship that doesn't serve me because I find the landscape of dating too hostile? The answer is still no.

I can only imagine that dating down is emotionally damaging. Never feeling truly happy and wondering what would have happened if you had decided to stay single. Some women come to this realisation after a few months, some years. How do we confront these issues? By dismantling stereotypes, I believe.

I used to always be ashamed when speaking to people about my dating preferences. I think it's fair to say that the conversation around interracial relationships is a somewhat touchy subject in the Black community. This is understandable, considering the historical tensions between white and black people because of centuries of slavery and segregation. You tell people you are open to dating different races and that you have in the past, and all they hear is: *'so you don't like Black men?'* *'You are anti-Black.'* *'It's giving self-hate.'*

So, some of you could imagine my frustration when a guy I had been dating for months looked at me across the dinner table and asked if I even liked Black men, because before him I had been papped with a white guy I was dating and I guess he couldn't quite get his head round it. I was more offended that he thought the 26-inch closure wig that I damn near broke my neck laying and the corseted dress that restricted my breathing was just to sit across from a person who I wasn't remotely attracted to.

'I can tell you only like white men,' he said with a cheeky grin on his face as if he had just unearthed my most intimate and shameful secret. For obvious reasons, it didn't quite work out between us.

I've only dated two white men (and I use the word 'dated' very loosely), one being a guy called Jake. Jake. I was obsessed with him. We met on Tinder and had made eye contact a few times in the student night clubs and even had mutual friends, but we didn't meet until my final year, my fourth Freshers' Week. He called my name while he was standing in the queue as my girlfriends and I were strutting our way into the night club. When we got in, he confessed that we had matched on Tinder. I played it down and pretended I didn't recognise him. The truth was his face was imprinted in my mind after countless Facebook searches and Instagram stalking. Over the next few weeks, we got on well and he invited me to watch a game with his housemates. Mind you, I hated football, but the thought of stealing a kiss was so worth the torture. I remember laughing so hard that day. Now I look back at it, I know whatever he said probably wasn't very funny, but he had a charm to him.

Randomly, I shouted across the room, 'Have you ever dated a Black girl before, Jake?' I wanted to figure out whether I was some sort of sick experiment, a fetish, or whether he just liked me. He broke a sweat as he turned to me, placed his hand in his pocket and answered very nonchalantly, 'No, I haven't, but I don't see colour.' I had smiled, thinking this was an acceptable answer. Later that night, we were left alone while his friends went out, hoping they would come back lucky. He stole a smile from my lips before tucking my 16-inch synthetic wig behind my ears and whispering, 'I've always been told Black girls really know how to work it.' I rolled my eyes in disgust and let out a heavy sigh. I had really liked this one. He looked up at me very confused, not understanding how those statements he made were not only degrading and insulting but were also a complete contradiction of one another. He was really on his bullshit, talking about 'love sees no colour' and at the same time fetishising me based on stereotypes about Black women he had absorbed while watching hip-hop music videos and porn.

So, let's take a minute and break down his statement of 'not seeing colour'. Reflecting on this now, all I can hear is a refusal to acknowledge my lived experiences as a Black woman along with the desire to stop discussing race, because it didn't make him feel comfortable. The failure to see colour forms the basis of a very considerable problem. It allows people to hide their real intentions, so they don't have to think about racism and confront their own prejudice. His statements were quite the misnomer. What he should have said was that he may not fully understand the challenges that an interracial relationship may face, but he was willing to learn and work it out together.

Having had these experiences while dating outside my

race doesn't change my stance on interracial relationships. However, I do believe that for this dynamic to work, it's important for your partner to be not only an advocate but an ally for your culture and community. It's crucial that you can be your real and authentic self with them. It would be quite naïve to limit your dating pool to only men within your race, especially if you are a Black woman. I mean, who among all races has statistically* been shown to date outside their race the most? No, I didn't pull this out of my ass, so don't @ me. This is not a tit-for-tat scenario; it's merely exploring your options and being open-minded enough to expand your horizons. It's about finding happiness and love in spaces that welcome you and that you are comfortable in.

One of the most valuable things I learnt this year was just to date. I know, it sounds easy, right? But for me this was the hardest thing I have had to do. To just date, and not to date with the preconception that this living human sitting in front of me could be my lifelong partner, to just date. Having food with strangers, finding out what I liked in the opposite sex and what I didn't. A real-life game of swiping left and right. I'll never forget one guy I dated who pulled his hoodie up and put his face mask on as we drove past an area in South London, because his 'ops were

---

* www.pewresearch.org/social-trends/2017/05/18/1-trends-and-patterns-in-intermarriage/

watching'. In that moment of time, I realised I wanted more for me and my homegirls. But that's not where my real revelation on what my expectations of my ideal partner was. It was when I met Jide, who also taught me the importance of dating when truly whole. I met Jide when my desire to love someone else overpowered my desire to love myself. I guess in a crazy way, I thought that by loving me, he would teach me how to love myself and *ooh boy* was I wrong. I was welcomed with disrespect and a love that was hostile and with conditions, blinded by the desire to feel an emotion I thought was love.

If I'm right, you might be thinking: *how do I know when I'm ready to date and how do I know that I'm whole? How do I know when to walk away and fall in love with myself first?* For years, I dated for all the wrong reasons: loneliness, boredom and superficial reasons that left me hollower and emptier from giving, giving and giving. The answer to that first question is not so straightforward. Everyone is different so the answer may vary but one thing that will remain constant is, you must first learn how to love yourself. I mean really love yourself, because I know you're THAT BITCH and you really need to believe that too. Forgive yourself for all the harsh and painful words you say to and about yourself. Find things that make you happy. Be genuinely content in your own solitude. Look for a partner because you want to enjoy life with them, not because you want them to fill a gap. When two people are in a relationship, it's evident when the love they share is respected, with boundaries, with desire to bring out the best in each other, because they have worked so hard to bring out the best in themselves. Walking away from a love you've grown accustomed to, a love that you *think* you deserve, can be quite challenging. I stayed with Jide for years, not because there was any love in the relationship but because at that time, I convinced myself that it was the closest thing to love I would ever have. I didn't know who I was without him, and I was terrified to find out. But finding the courage to walk away was one of my greatest achievements when navigating the dating scene. Like most of you reading this chapter, I know I'm not alone when I say one of the biggest betrayals to a woman, especially while dating, is trust. And that's exactly what Jide did when he welcomed other women to our monogamous relationship.

I'm ashamed to admit I was aware of his infidelities. I turned a blind eye to the women who messaged him late at night, the last-minute cancellations and the distance between us. At the time it was easy to blame the culture I was surrounded by and the voices that drowned my mind. *'Every man cheats. You just have to find one that's worth staying for.' 'Are you really going to leave your man because he cheated lol?'* were the reactions I got when I informed the girls at uni about Jide and his relationships with girls I called my friends, exes and random women he spoke to for a couple of seconds at the bar, just because he could. A quick example of normalising the infidelities of Black men. Of course, I remained faithful like a submissive Nigerian woman, but let's be honest here, that's not the real reason. I had lost myself so much that I didn't know who I was without Jide. I didn't stay because I loved him and I felt like I couldn't live without him. I stayed because I didn't know what life was without him. I forgot what solitude felt like; I feared my own loneliness. I was lost, confused and I feared the unknown. With each day, I could see pieces of myself slipping away, pieces of myself I loved, pieces of myself my friends and family recognised. I was now unrecognisable. I had succeeded in losing myself fully. I could see myself falling down this continuous dark tunnel with no lifeline and no way out, but all I had to do was open my eyes and see. See that what I had to do was choose me, walk away, and heal. It wasn't easy, but I did it. What was the result? Growth, happiness and love. So, here's to us being terrified, but taking that leap of faith and doing it anyway.

* * *

A few words from me to you . . .

To whom it may concern,

Hey, hi, it's me again. Not only do you deserve a love that is unapologetically genuine, true, unfiltered and rich in its embrace, but you also deserve to love yourself as equally.

Don't be worried when you cannot find someone to dance to the beat that your heart so carefully curated with every string and drum; it was designed precisely by you, for only a few to understand.

Never dim down the intensity of your love to make others accept it. You are perfect just how you are. I promise it's not too much.

There's no need to rush. There is no need to compromise. The love you deserve will come.

I hope you haven't watered down your love and it is still as strong as a glass of neat scotch on a cold winter's night and as gentle as silk linen. I hope they haven't broken your love, but if they have, I hope you mend the cracks with golden flecks of self-love.

Above all, I hope YOU always choose happiness.

To the Men Who Were Careless with My Love,

You were careless with my love, not because you were devious in your calculations, but because I was devious in mine. I searched for souls who were nurturers, who like me were half full, in hopes we could make each other whole. I now realise how selfish that was. And for that, I apologise, but I refuse to apologise for opening my heart and loving you without restrictions.

I read so many books and learnt all the languages of

love but failed to learn the most important one: the language of self-love. I am no longer willing to save a sinking ship on my own. I choose me. I choose me. I must save myself.

The woman you knew is gone. I have changed and evolved like a snake shedding old skin. I have been born again.

I left, not because I wanted to, but because I had to. I had to love myself enough to leave. I would have been doing myself a great injustice to stay. A disservice to my own growth and healing.

Contrary to what you may believe, I am no longer resentful of you. I don't regret meeting you; I don't regret loving you.

Our paths were precisely aligned, the universe wanted us to find each other. To share a different type of love, a platonic love. A love that would allow us to learn and grow from each other.

Thank you for the lessons you taught me. I didn't realise how much I had lost myself in you.

To My Future Lover,

I no longer fantasise over a love I must fight for, a love in which I constantly have to echo my worth, a love in which I am constantly disrespected and ignored. I am nobody's ride or die. I no longer settle for hollow love. I fantasise over a love that is infectious, a love in which we are both synchronised to the same rhythm. A love that blossoms and does not just exist. A love with respectable boundaries.

Be patient with my love, I am unlearning bad habits that too many old lovers taught me. Be careful with my love, it's fragile. I've only recently learnt how to love myself. I'm learning how to love better you too.

I need a love that is intoxicating but still allows me to come up for air, to breathe, to reflect and to grow. I like my love to be honest, uncomplicated, peaceful, vulnerable and sweet.

My love for you will never overshadow the love I have for myself; I have worked too hard to let that happen. I hope you can understand.

Chapter Nine: Pass Me My Lab Coat

'When I grow up, I'm going to be a doctor, or a scientist.'
'Haha, don't be silly. That's not a girl's job.'

When you look at me, what do you see? Do you see an entrepreneur, a writer, an academic with two degrees in life and physical sciences? A scientist? Assuming your answer was yes, when you think of a scientist, do you still see me, or do you see an image of a nerdy white man in a lab coat performing (what I now know to be) an inorganic experiment? Or do you see *me*, a young Black woman with a lab coat smiling right at you, wearing bifocal lenses arched over the brim of my nose?

Okay, but what if I said technology, engineering and maths. What do you see? Do you still see me? If your answer is no for most of these questions, I want you to ask yourself why? Is it because STEM (Science, Technology, Engineering and Maths) is a male-dominated industry and in that respect the media does a fantastic job of portraying it? Or is the casual misogyny, something that is overlooked far too quickly sometimes in an industry like this, simply ignored? So, it doesn't take me by surprise when these messages are perpetuated in society. Whether we like it or not the media does impact our real-life perception of the world around us. With that in mind, I set myself on a journey to reclaim, redefine and rediversify an image of what a scientist looked like.

I didn't always see myself in science. If you would've asked me a decade or two ago what I wanted to be when I was older, I would have said, an actress, a TV presenter or maybe in a girl group. I was always too shy to be on my own and it would also mask the fact that I couldn't actually hold a note, even if you paid me. Being the first-born child to first-generation immigrant parents meant that I had my whole life planned out before the age of one. I became this bundle of hope and a chance to live a life that they both dreamt of, not only for me but for themselves. A life full of academia and what they described as a 'respectable career', something they could brag about when they were updating their family and friends back home. So, it's no surprise they raised a scientist, a software engineer, a nurse and a doctor. My parents sent three out of four of us to primary school at the age of three. So, I was ready for university by the age of sixteen.

'You don't just have to be great, you have to be extraordinary,' my mother would shout while performing household duties, as if someone had whispered that we had been dreaming of rolling out on the fields instead of getting ahead on next year's curriculum. 'I don't want anyone to say, I came to their country and all I did was take. That's why I work so hard. That's why you must too.' She said these words repeatedly. Each time the corners of her eyes creased with concern, as I watched the emotions bloom in her face, chest and stomach.

My parents would always remind me about my older cousins and their friends' children who had been high achievers in their school and showed signs of a successful career. They always did so in the most passive aggressive manner.

'YEWANDE, did you hear, your cousin in Canada has graduated from med school?' my mum chirped while dancing with joy.

'Your own time is coming, we will celebrate your good news too!' my dad added eagerly, as I stood still with a blank expression.

'Are you not going to say Amen?' they shouted in a harmonious synchronisation, marking me with a poisonous gaze.

I quickly realised when it came to career paths, the choice certainly wasn't mine. I took a seat and was faced with the realisation that I had to choose a career that not only intrigued me but was on the very short list of professional occupations that were acceptable for a Nigerian woman.

'You can be a lawyer, a doctor or even an engineer. You know Yinka's dad, he didn't have any boys, but he was blessed enough to still have an engineer and an architect,' my dad rambled on. But what he didn't know was he somehow managed to break the gender gap society had placed me in when exploring career perspectives, although his intentions were far from altruistic. It ignited a flame I didn't want to put out. I wanted to be extraordinary, I wanted to break boundaries and make a contribution to the world before I left.

I always had an interest in the things I couldn't understand. Like how two hydrogen atoms fused with an oxygen molecule created water and was somehow now a stable compound. But I had a science teacher who made me feel like it was her life's mission to keep me stagnant and remind me that I would never be good enough and that I didn't belong in her class.

'Yewande, I just don't think this class is for you. Have you had much thought on what subjects you wanna sit for the leaving cert?' she inquired emotionlessly, while whipping the chalk off the blackboard.

'No Miss, I really like this class. I can work harder.' There was a note of desperation in my voice.

I didn't really know what she expected from me considering my grades were immaculate and I had never failed an exam in my life.

'Well, if you don't want to change, maybe we should talk about sitting an ordinary level exam and maybe dropping science all together for the leaving cert.'

I felt a wash of despair, but I managed to pick myself up. 'No Miss, I'm just going to stick with higher level,' I mumbled, my eyes fixated on the dirt on my shoes, too afraid to look up.

'Sure look, it's your choice. I just don't know if you're going to pass the exam.'

By now some of you will know that I didn't take her advice. I passed my exam with a distinction and ended up choosing biology and chemistry as choice subjects for my leaving cert, but it was the micro-inequity she instilled in me that was damaging – a moment that stuck with me forever. An encounter I later realised was just the start of my unconventional journey as a Black woman in STEM.

I don't think there was a specific moment that catapulted me into the field of physical sciences; unfortunately I didn't have a light bulb moment or a strange calling from the sky telling me it was my one and only destiny. It was more like a collection of moments. I've always been a naturally inquisitive person and my interest lay specifically in biology. I was fascinated by the 'how' and 'why' and had an urge to somehow turn my answers to biological solutions to help patients or add to scientific research. Of course, I had other interests – my more creative side. But it was something I was too scared to pursue for fear that I would enjoy it and it would be taken away because it was a hobby and not a career, according to my parents. And of course, the two could never become one. So, I chose to study biotechnology, an area of biology where living systems are used to manufacture beneficial biological products, for example insulin for diabetics.

Because my parents were so keen on the idea of me studying science, engineering, medicine or law, it came to me as a surprise when I was the only Black girl in my university lecture, that I saw no Black science lecturers, no Black female lab demonstrators, and the only representation I had was myself. I wondered where all the first-generation children who had been practically groomed to take up spaces in this lecture room were. Over time, it created this white-structured notion of inferiority, which led to me questioning my mental capabilities. Due to the lack of representation, I couldn't see myself as a scientist. I didn't know where I belonged, what a career for me in an industry that was already male-and-white dominated actually looked like. Even when my exam results reflected that I was more than capable. I found myself working harder, constantly trying to prove that I was deserving of my space. Then downplaying my achievements because they weren't expected of me. *'Baffles me how you pass your exams, it does. Like, how the fuck did you do better than me?'* were constant reminders in my lecture room from other students. So, it was no surprise when Imposter Syndrome came knocking at my door. They were right, I didn't know what I was doing and why I was there. I felt like a fraud.

I suddenly felt like I had all these roadblocks in front of me that I didn't know how to get by. Not only am I trying to navigate the oppressive systems I'm faced with because I'm from a marginalised community. I also have to break down stereotypes of a Black woman's intellect and deal with Imposter Syndrome because of it. Something people who aren't from marginalised communities don't even have to think about. A seed that was planted throughout my second level education and seamlessly continued into my third level education, it inculcated additional ideas of inferiority that were perpetuated by the lack of support in lectures and harsh and incorrect markings in exams.

'Ciara, d'ya reckon these were marked a bit harsh? I thought I did class in this,' I prodded, leaning forward in an attempt to see her score.

'Happy with mine, I thought I would've done so much worse,' she said laughing, mesmerised by the score on her phone.

'Ermm I just feel a bit shit. This is the only lecture I feel my efforts just don't reflect in my marks. I dunno maybe I'm just being silly,' I confessed, expressing my concern.

'Sure, send him an email and say it to him, then,' Ciara responded boldly, surprised that I hadn't done so already.

I guess I kinda felt intimidated by the lecturer and the process of demanding the marks I knew I not only deserved but had earned. Because by doing that I would be indirectly calling out his implicit bias and lack of professionalism. I was also scared he would see through my charade, that maybe I wasn't as intelligent as I thought I was, that he was in fact, generous with his marks and I was making a big mistake. But it was too late, he had already opened the door. I detected a sense of incredulity when I showed up to his office and requested we both go through my manuscript to highlight areas I clearly seemed to be struggling with.

'I don't see any corrections for this paragraph – was I totally off point here?' I queried.

His eyes fluttered a few beats. 'Oooh I didn't see this.' His voice was stiff and prim. He turned over the manu-script, exposing at least two pages of work he hadn't bothered correcting. He quickly grabbed a pen in an attempt to rectify the situation. I wondered why he thought I wasn't deserving of the marks in the first place; was mine the only paper that wasn't marked correctly? Did he question my intelligence or was it just an honest mistake? I got into the habit of constantly proving people wrong, especially male mentors who told me I couldn't graduate with first class because they had fallen short. *'A first class? That's ambitious. They don't give those out very often. I didn't get one, so maybe don't get your hopes set too high.'*

So, it wasn't a surprise that I was met with this same hostility after three years of working in the biopharma-ceutical industry. Jumping through hoops of sexism, racism, biases and isolation in the workplace. You know, just the normal hurdles of being a Black woman in a predominantly white and male industry. However, what took me by surprise was that some of these feelings were perpetrated towards me by another Black woman in my department. She spent the time she should have used advancing her career to compete with me because we'd both been taught that there was only one seat at the table for people who looked like us. So instead of uplifting each other, we competed, tore each other down through lies and sabotage till there was only one woman standing. It started with reassigning my laboratory test to herself and with me purposely communicating incorrect meeting times so her absence suggested incompetence. It's ludicrous to expect Black women and other ethnic minorities to remain in work environments where they cannot grow and thrive. Spaces where we aren't seen as qualified members of the team but anomalies. We also cannot expect girls to enter fields where they do not see positive representation. We need more women from a diverse range of backgrounds to be given opportunities and support to take up leadership positions in STEM industries. This will provide a much-needed shift in race and gender representation, which is vital have to encourage more girls (especially Black girls) into these fields. . It's true what they say, *'you can't be what you can't see'*. I had high expectations for my career and dreamt of one day being head of a department. I had never seen it achieved by any Black woman in Ireland, and it was important for me to rediversify this image. And that's why this chapter is so important to me to write.

So now that I find myself in a creative career, it's challenging, but pivotal. I now have to programme my mind to think outside the box. To switch from an analytical to a synthetic thinker, an invaluable skill I learnt because I stepped outside the box I placed myself in. There isn't a day that doesn't go by without someone asking if 'I'm still a scientist'. The answer to your question is yes, even though I'm not in the industry at the moment. STEM is a lifestyle, hun! After spending five years in university and countless hours in the library, I would like to think so. However, I do hope that when the time comes that I decide to switch things up again, the skills I've acquired in my creative career will give me an innovative edge.

I came across a crazy statistic from the European Institute of Gender Equality* that said closing the gender gap in STEM would inversely contribute to the EU GDP per capita by 2.2 to 3.0% by 2050. What does that mean for the economy? It means MORE MONEY! An improvement in GDP by €610 to €820 billion by 2050. The fact remains that we simply aren't doing enough to attract

---

* https://eige.europa.eu/gender-mainstreaming/policy-areas/economic -and-financial-affairs/economic-benefits-gender-equality

young girls and women to areas in STEM, even though many would argue that the mere numerical underrepresentation of women or Black women in this discipline is simply from a lack of interest. I would argue that it's from lack of representation and due to the implicit, unconscious or unintentional bias against women. That implicit bias sometimes is more damaging than the stereotypes themselves. I don't know how many times I have to say it, but a scientist does not equate to a man in a white lab coat. Without change and adequate representation across all media channels, we won't be able to produce an army of engineers or scientists at the very time in our nation's history when we're under increasing pressure to maintain an innovative edge and increasing demand to solve complex, challenging scientific and technical problems. We need a diverse team of people of different genders, races and socioeconomic classes from different parts of the world. When it comes to innovative solutions to a really challenging problem then a diverse team will trump a team of experts every time. So, if we want solutions to global crises and technological advancements, we all have to work at getting the message out to our girls that not only can they do science, technology, engineering and maths, we need them in these disciplines. We need to help them achieve their dreams and use their skills to make the world a better place because the dreams of that young girl in school are the key to building our future.

Maintaining your sense of self in a world that is not supportive of you is difficult, but not impossible. There will be hurdles and roadblocks that you will have to navigate simply because you're a woman. Unfortunately, we don't yet live in a world that doesn't centre around heteropatriarchy. The impact these educational institutions have, whether conscious or unconscious, insidiously slows down the progress of women in STEM. Collectively, we have the power to dismantle heteropatriarchal systems and accomplish real change. Until then, strive for greatness, be extraordinary and don't be afraid to be an anomaly. There will be times when you will be the only person in the room who looks and sounds like you. Don't silence yourself, speak loudly, speak with authority, let your voice be heard. You deserve to be in that room. You are deserving of those roles you feel you are not deserving of. You've worked hard for them. Don't let your gender or race hold you back. Whatever career you choose to follow, don't just be great, be extraordinary. Not because you feel the need to always prove yourself to others but because you owe it to yourself to achieve your fullest capabilities. I grew up with the mindset that you could only have one successful career in one particular field. But that's far from the truth. I'm a writer, a content creator, an entrepreneur. There's no novelty without creativity – explore every facet of your being.

Final Thoughts

'A book with empty pages waiting to be written . . .'

A letter to my future self – trust me, I got you.

I wasn't sure how to start this. I looked at the empty page on my screen for hours and hours before my laptop forced itself into standby mode and I was startled by my own reflection. A round-headed human staring at me with judgemental eyes, wearing a hydrating face mask and holding a glass of non-alcoholic wine. Writing this book has been a pivotal moment in my life, it forced me to pause, reflect, grow, heal, take advantage of my strengths and challenge my weaknesses. It helped me find myself and guided me on the right path to becoming a better version of me. A version I always aspired to be growing up. I have a long way to go on this journey, but I guess this is where it starts. With this commitment, these words and this letter I write here today, to my future self, but also maybe to you too.

You let fear and people's opinions of you hold you back from exploring the best parts of you. No more making decisions based on everyone's expectations of you, and just *be*. Enough hiding versions of yourself to accommodate everyone's expectations of who you are. When there's still so many versions to be awakened. Stop chasing others' footprints and create ones unique to you and your journey. It may seem scary, unpredictable and out of control at first, but I promise it will be worth it in the end. We are no longer measuring your strengths based on the strengths of others and fearing failure. My biggest fear was that my flaws were too hideous to be overlooked, flaws that have been left behind by those who were careless with my love. The best moments happen in the blink of an eye when you just let go, so we are over trying to control things we can't change! Control is overrated anyways, well at least that's what I'm telling myself now. Stop romanticising perfection, an illusion created by the human mind to keep us bound, fixated in our own minds and continuously striving for unrealistic goals that will never be met. You have spent so much time daydreaming and not enough time living your dreams, being present and making memories. Life is so precious, each day isn't promised, grab life by the balls and never let them go!

I hope you've learnt not to take life too seriously; I hope each day from now on is filled with laughter. I hope your laugh is as loud as a hungry lion. I hope it fills your lungs with air and leaves a permanent smile on your face. I hope you find true happiness. I hope you've learnt not to derive your happiness from your relationships. I hope you're able to share your joy with others.

Let go of that Scorpio energy, girrrlll, it's not worth it and it's very draining! Stop holding onto grudges, let your guard down a little – anyone who taught you anything about life or yourself was a blessing in disguise. Your paths were always aligned; the universe either wants you to learn one of the many lessons life loves to teach or it surrounds you with the right people to help you be the best version of yourself. Let go of all that toxic energy habituating in your heart chambers and fill it with love, happiness and hopes for the future.

I have no desire to remain stagnant; I have no desire to not know growth. I am not the same person I was yester-day, and I will never apologise for that. I will continue striving to break out of boxes society has put me in.

Being an introvert has had its benefits; it has allowed me to nurture my internal relationship and protect my peace. But now it's time to learn to be comfortable in uncomfortable situations. Step out of my comfort zone.

I was taught to love with conditions, that love was only given as a reward. I chased the love I thought I was deserving of because I was taught that love was some-thing you had to fight for, something you had to earn, and only after I proved myself worthy, while losing a little bit of me in the process, could I be rewarded with a love that was half empty. Parts of me are still learning that I deserve a love I don't have to fight for. I deserve a love that has no bounds, like an ocean constantly flowing, like a harmonious orchestra but fierce in its waves of affection, sweeping along unpredicted paths. How naïve I was to think I could make these changes overnight. How naïve I was to think that choosing me and not a love with conditions was selfish. I want you to learn how to practise true self-love and not let your past experiences with love define how you love yourself and future lovers.

Be protective of your energy, be protective of your soul and be protective of your space. Be grateful for the journey old friends lead you on and aware of those who camouflage their bitterness and jealousy as kindness and love have left. They've made room for others to occupy your heart and fill it with joy and happiness. I hope the people you have in your life now bring you inner peace.

So, from this day on I commit to growth, healing and selflessness in always choosing myself. I hope you've learnt that you don't have to cover your scars out of shame. Who taught you to be ashamed? Habits that are learnt can easily be unlearnt. I hope you are on your way to unlearning them. I hope you're at a stage in your life where your happiness and wellbeing are your first priority. You've poured so much into others, constantly giving and giving, until your barrel was empty, it's time to start pouring back into yourself. Be intentional with your healing, never place this responsibility on anyone else. I'm leaving my old self behind and I'm so excited to meet future you.

Look how far you've come over the years!

With love,

Yewande (the one you used to know) X

Acknowledgements

I wrote the first draft of this multiple times in my head before I was able to put pen to paper. I acknowledged everyone under the sun except for myself. So, I scrapped it all and started again. We live in such a busy century where we fail to pause and take in moments. We rush through life trying so desperately to get to the finish line, the brighter horizon, the pot of gold at the end of the rainbow, without taking time to appreciate the small moments, the big accomplishments and the learning blocks we picked up along the way. So, I want to take this time to acknowledge the pain, the laughter and the perseverance that has brought me this far.

To the version of me who was so scared to speak, be heard and be seen. I hope you're proud of the person you've become and the voice that is now too loud to be tamed.

To you, my precious reader, thank you for choosing to go on this journey with me. I hope it was everything you wanted it to be. This book would not be possible without you. You helped me find myself and my voice. It all started with a note I wrote on my iPhone and posted on

Twitter. Articles I wrote that you got behind. For all your support. I'm forever grateful.

To the Mushens Entertainment and Hodder publishing teams, the road certainly hasn't been easy, but thank you for taking the leap of faith, believing in me, nurturing my talent and bringing this book to life. For that I will always be grateful. Thank you for always diverging me to the road not taken and holding my hand when it got dark, and I could no longer see the light at the end of a bright tunnel.

To my secondary school English teacher Miss Butler, whose impact has been like no other. Thank you for your drive, commitment and the endless quotes you made me learn. Thank you for making me the writer I am today. You're the reason every chapter begins with a quote.

To my friends and family, your eyes, voice and heart gave me the courage to write this book, to finish this book. Your love gave me the confidence to believe that not only could I write, I was damn good at it too. Thanks for shading the cast of self-doubt and fear when its shadow became too unbearable to mask.

To my sister Ayobami, to whom this book is dedicated, who is forever in my heart and walks by my side every day. I feel you here and I hope you are proud of the voice you hear. I love and miss you every day.

Thank you all x